# My Name is Lucy Barton: A Guide for Book Clubs

KATHRYN COPE

Copyright © 2016 Kathryn Cope

All rights reserved.

ISBN: 1532733186
ISBN-13: 978-1532733185

## CONTENTS

| | | |
|---|---|---|
| 1 | Introduction | 1 |
| 2 | *My Name is Lucy Barton* | 3 |
| 3 | Elizabeth Strout | 5 |
| 4 | Plot summary | 8 |
| 5 | Style | 23 |
| 6 | Themes & Imagery | 25 |
| 7 | Characters | 41 |
| 8 | Discussion questions | 61 |
| 9 | Quiz | 65 |
| 10 | Further reading | 69 |
| 11 | Bibliography | 71 |

# INTRODUCTION

There are few things more rewarding than getting together with a group of like-minded people and discussing a good book. Book club meetings, at their best, are vibrant, passionate affairs. Each member will bring along a different perspective and ideally there will be heated debate.

A surprising number of book club members, however, report that their meetings have been a disappointment. Even though their group loved the particular book they were discussing, they could think of astonishingly little to say about it. Failing to find interesting discussion angles for a book is the single most common reason for book group discussions to fall flat. Most book groups only meet once a month and a lacklustre meeting is frustrating for everyone.

The Reading Room Book Group Guides were born out of a passion for book clubs. Packed with information, they take the hard work out of preparing for a meeting and ensure that your book group discussions never run dry. How you choose to use the guides is entirely up to you. The author biography and literary style sections provide useful background information which may be interesting to share with your group at the beginning of your meeting. The all-important list of discussion questions, which will probably form the core of your meeting, can be found towards the end of this guide. To support your responses to the discussion questions, you may find it helpful to refer to the 'Themes & Imagery' and 'Character' sections.

A detailed plot synopsis is provided as an *aide-memoire* if you need to recap on the finer points of the plot. There is also a quick quiz - a fun way to test your knowledge and bring your discussion to a close. Finally, if this was a book that you particularly enjoyed, the guide concludes with a list of books similar in style or subject matter.

Be warned, this guide contains spoilers. Please do not be tempted to read it before you have read the original novel as plot surprises will be well and truly ruined.

Kathryn Cope, 2016

# *MY NAME IS LUCY BARTON* BY ELIZABETH STROUT

As the title of Elizabeth Strout's novel strongly suggests, *My Name is Lucy Barton* reads very much like a memoir. With the perspective of hindsight, the eponymous protagonist describes a nine-week period in the 1980s which she spent in hospital. After having her appendix removed in a straightforward operation, Lucy falls mysteriously ill and undergoes a series of tests at the instruction of her concerned doctor. Feeling isolated and pining for her two daughters, Lucy is astonished and delighted when her estranged mother makes the long journey to visit her and stays for five days and nights. During her visit, they mainly talk about the lives of women from their hometown of Amgash, Illinois. While these conversations seem to bring mother and daughter together, they also circle around the many things that are unsayable about their family history which, Lucy slowly reveals, involves poverty, neglect and abuse.

At first glance, *My Name is Lucy Barton* might be mistaken for a small book both in size and scope. On beginning to read it, however, it quickly becomes apparent to the reader that this is an ordinary story told in an extraordinary manner. While the momentum of the novel is driven by a series of anecdotes rather than an all-consuming plot, the apparently everyday moments that Lucy describes are charged with significance. Powerful, subtle and affecting, this slim novel expresses more about the nature of being human than many much weightier tomes.

Much of this novel's emotional power stems from its strongly autobiographical feel. Lucy's first-person voice is inviting and engaging and feels utterly authentic. Readers get to know her by piecing all her little anecdotes together, in the same way they would get to know a friend. Although damaged and vulnerable, Lucy is also surprisingly optimistic and possesses a generous heart. After finishing the novel, many readers will mourn her absence from their lives.

For book groups there are also huge themes to discuss here, including the complexity of mother-daughter relationships; loneliness; social exclusion; class; the nature of love, and the purpose of fiction. For a little book about a relatively ordinary life, *My Name is Lucy Barton* packs an incredibly powerful punch.

# ELIZABETH STROUT

## Life

Elizabeth Strout is a Pulitzer Prize-winning American novelist, short story writer and academic. Born in 1956 in Portland, Maine, she was raised by strict parents who were both academics. Following her graduation from a liberal arts college in Maine, Strout went on to law school. After practising as "an awful, awful lawyer for six months", however, Strout realised that it was not the profession for her and returned to her first love - writing. Her reputation as a writer slowly grew with the publication of a number of short stories and then her first novel in 1998. Strout only became a household name, however, with the publication of *Olive Kitteridge* in 2008 which won the Pulitzer Prize for fiction. Strout currently lives in Manhattan.

## Work

While Strout's five published novels vary in subject matter, they have certain elements in common. Several are set in small towns in New England and explore similar themes: family dynamics; loneliness; social judgement; grief and childhood fears. As a writer, Strout is essentially interested in character and her great strength is a resistance to sentimentality. Strout's novels portray the nature of human experience in a subtle and truthful way through characters who are flawed and all the more human for it. In her own words, "It is not 'good' or 'bad' that interests me as a writer, but the murkiness of human experience and consistent imperfections of our lives."

### *Amy and Isabelle* (1998)

In Strout's first novel, the title characters are a daughter and mother who share a tense love-hate relationship. When sixteen-year-old Amy is caught having sex with her teacher in a car, her mother, Isabelle, has to face the town's gossip which brings back shameful memories of her own.

### *Abide with Me* (2006)

Strout's second novel focuses upon Reverend Tyler Caskey, a minister in a small New England town in the 1950s. The story follows the minster's life after the tragic death of his young wife. While he continues to listen to the woes of his parishioners, Strout movingly illustrates how Tyler is privately struggling to cope with his own grief, family life, and loss of faith.

### *Olive Kitteridge* (2008)

Strout's Pulitzer Prize-winning novel is really a collection of thirteen short stories, all set in the same New England town and all linked by the presence of the title character. In each story Strout recounts the hopes and thwarted desires of a different resident of the small fictional town of Crosby. Running through all these accounts (sometimes as a major character and sometimes only mentioned as an aside) is Olive Kitteridge, a formidable retired schoolteacher, notorious for her blunt, abrasive manner. On closer examination, however, Olive is not as monstrous as she first appears. By slowly revealing the desires and emotions concealed by Olive beneath her brusque exterior, Strout presents a poignant portrait of a woman who feels both love and compassion but cannot express it. Following the great success of this novel, it was adapted into an acclaimed Emmy-winning TV series starring Frances McDormand.

### *The Burgess Boys* (2013)

When Jim and Bob Burgess are boys they are present when their father is killed in an accident so awful that the family never speaks about it. Later, eager to escape their Maine hometown of Shirley

Falls, both brothers become lawyers in New York. While Jim, the confident brother, becomes a wealthy corporate lawyer, the more compassionate Bob works as a legal aid attorney. Both brothers find their lives disrupted when they are contacted by their sister, Susan, who begs for their professional help after her teenage son commits a shocking hate crime. As they return to Shirley Falls to do what they can for their nephew, the brothers find that buried tensions and resentments soon erupt between them. Like a number of Strout's other works, this novel explores family dynamics and the festering presence of the unsaid.

# PLOT

While the main core of the novel centres upon the five days when Lucy's mother visits her in hospital, its narrative is by no means chronological. Writing about her mother's visit triggers other memories for Lucy that fall both before and after the event. These memories are interspersed throughout the narrative. The following summary traces the train of Lucy's memories in the order that they appear in the novel.

## **Summary**

Lucy Barton recalls a time many years ago, in the mid-1980s, when she had to stay in a New York hospital for nearly nine weeks.

After going into hospital for a routine appendix removal, Lucy develops a fever. Unable to establish the cause, the hospital doctor keeps her in for tests. When she is first admitted, Lucy is placed in a room next to a dying old woman who keeps calling out for help. Her husband then pays to have Lucy moved to a private room which has a view of the Chrysler building. Although the cries of the dying woman distressed her, Lucy feels lonely in her private room and desperately misses her two young daughters.

Lucy's husband rarely has the time to visit her. One day, however, a family friend brings her daughters in to see her. Lucy's girls are subdued and she notices that the family friend, who has no children of her own, has forgotten to brush their hair and wash their faces.

Three weeks into her stay, Lucy finds her mother sitting at the foot of her hospital bed. As she hasn't seen her mother for years, she is astonished that she would have flown many miles to see her. Lucy finds her mother's presence hugely comforting and sleeps through the night for the first time since she has been ill.

Lucy's mother is still by her bedside in the morning and stays for five nights in all, only ever sleeping in her chair. She asks after Lucy's daughters but never mentions Lucy's husband, William (who Lucy later finds out was responsible for calling her mother and paying for her flight). Neither of the women mentions Lucy's father, although they talk about her siblings. Lucy's brother, who is in his mid-thirties, is jobless and still living with his parents. Lucy's mother also reveals that he sleeps in a barn with animals due to be slaughtered the next day. Lucy's older sister is married with five children and lives ten miles away from her parents. The women also discuss the hospital nurses and give them all nicknames: Cookie, Toothache and Serious Child.

Lucy's mother moves on to telling stories about people from their hometown. Lucy asks her mother to tell the story of Kathie Nicely. Her mother relates how one of her customers, Kathie Nicely, left her husband, two daughters and comfortable home for another man. As soon as she abandoned her family, however, her lover dropped her. As a result, Kathie ended up living in a small apartment on her own, as her husband and daughters never forgave her. After her mother finishes the story, Lucy becomes upset at the thought of Kathie Nicely's fate and declares that her husband should have taken her back.

Lucy explains to the reader that her family were "oddities" in their hometown of Amgash, Illinois and lived on the outskirts, isolated from other people. As a consequence, Lucy's only 'friend' was a single tree that grew in the middle of a nearby cornfield. At school, Lucy and her sister, Vicky, were scorned by teachers and classmates alike for being dirty and smelly. Their father was in and out of work repairing farm machinery, while their mother took in sewing. Supper frequently consisted of molasses on bread and Lucy was often "ravenous". Their parents - especially their mother – often hit the children "impulsively and vigorously". With no access to TV, books or newspapers, Lucy and her siblings were ignorant of what the rest of the world was like or how they should behave in it. Later in life, Lucy often tries to convince herself that her childhood was not so bad. At other times, however, she is overcome by terror when she thinks about it and, as a remedy, tries to strike up conversations with strangers.

Lucy and her family lived in a garage until she was eleven years old. The garage belonged to her great-uncle who lived in the house next door. When the uncle died, they moved into the house which was more spacious but still very cold. Lucy often stayed late at school to do her homework and read books to keep warm. When she reached the third grade, she read a book about two middle-class girls whose mother teaches them to be nice to a poor and dirty little girl called Tilly. The book made Lucy feel less lonely and she decided that she would become a writer to make other people feel "less alone". For many years, however, she kept her ambition secret, even from her husband.

In high school Lucy got excellent grades and, with no encouragement from her parents, went to college on a scholarship. While she was there, she had a brief affair with a professor who was also an artist. Lucy fell in love with him and even respected his decision to forego having children in order to pursue his art. She also tried to overlook his unexpected superficiality, demonstrated by the disparaging comments he made about Lucy's thrift store clothes and by his boasts about buying a shirt from Bloomingdale's. One day, however, he made a crass remark about the poverty of her childhood and she realised that there was no future for them.

Lucy's husband, William, is the son of a German prisoner of war. They met at college and when they got engaged, William wanted to meet Lucy's parents and tell them of their plans to marry. When Lucy's father met William, however, he became agitated and made it clear that his future son-in-law was unwelcome. Recognising the signs, Lucy feared that her father was going to have one of the anxiety episodes she refers to as 'the Thing'. As they hurriedly left, Lucy's mother blamed her daughter for not warning them about William's ancestry, claiming that some German men tried to kill her father in the war. Years later, however, Lucy's brother reveals the truth: that their father shot two young German civilians in the back during WWII and was plagued with guilt for the rest of his life. When he met William, he was reminded of one of those young men and thought he had come for revenge.

Lucy's family did not attend or acknowledge her wedding and, after that point, Lucy only called them on special occasions and on the birth of her daughters, Christina and Becka.

In the hospital, Lucy asks her mother why Kathie Nicely's lover let her down. Her mother says that the man in question later confessed to Kathie that he was a "homo". Lucy laughs and her mother reluctantly joins in. She feels real joy in being able to talk to her mother in this new, intimate way.

Lucy and William live in the West Village in an apartment block. In the same building, Lucy has a friend called Jeremy who she is "half in love" with. One day Lucy locked herself out of her apartment with the children and their dog and Jeremy invited her into his sophisticated apartment. One of Lucy's daughters told Jeremy that her mother had just had a story published in a magazine. Lucy made light of the achievement but Jeremy took her seriously, telling her that, as an artist, she will have to be "ruthless". On another occasion, Lucy confided to Jeremy that she almost envied the increasing number of young men suffering from AIDS on the streets of New York, "because they have each other". Jeremy looked at her with sympathy, seeming to understand her loneliness.

One day, several years after her stay in hospital, Lucy goes into an expensive clothes store and is immediately drawn to a stylish, older woman. Lucy strikes up a conversation with her and asks her name and what she does for a living. Embarrassed, the woman reluctantly tells Lucy that her name is Sarah Payne and that she is "just a writer". When Lucy gets home she realises that she has read and enjoyed some of Sarah Payne's novels which focus on the lives of ordinary rural people. She also remembers that she once met a man at a party who criticised Sarah's work for its "softness of compassion".

At the hospital, Lucy tells her mother that she is worried about her sleeping only in the chair. Her mother replies that she learned to take 'cat naps' early on in her life: a useful skill "when you don't feel safe." Lucy realises she knows very little about her mother's childhood and wonders what she was scared of.

Lucy's mother tells her daughter about the summers she spent as a child on a farm belonging to her Aunt Celia. Her companion there was her cousin, Harriet, who she describes as "silly" due to her fear of everything from lightning to snakes. At the mention of snakes, Lucy becomes distressed and asks her mother not to use that word.

At Lucy's request, her mother tells the story of Harriet's "poor luck". According to Lucy's mother, Harriet struggled to stop her children being taken into care after her husband unexpectedly died. Later, Harriet's daughter, Dottie, also suffered bad luck in her marriage when her husband ran off with someone he met when he was having his gallbladder removed. Both women recall Harriet's son, Abel Blaine, with great affection. Lucy remembers that the local children used to laugh at Abel as his trousers were always too short, but he remained cheerful and taught her how to hunt for food in the dumpster behind the cake shop. Her mother tells Lucy that Abel went on to marry the daughter of his boss and now lives a comfortable life in Chicago. Lucy realises that she is desperate to tell her mother about her own life and blurts out that she has had two stories published in magazines. Her mother doesn't respond and looks out of the window. Lucy then asks her mother why she didn't feel safe as a child. Her mother closes her eyes and again doesn't reply.

While she is in hospital, Lucy develops a deep attachment to her Jewish doctor who treats her with a tender care that goes well beyond professional requirements. Lucy thinks about the doctor for many years afterwards and donates money to the hospital in his name.

Lucy remembers the terrifying occasions when she was locked inside her father's truck as a small child. Sometimes she would be locked in because her parents were out at work and sometimes as a punishment. On each occasion, she would scream and bang on the windows.

Apart from Jeremy, Lucy's only other friend in the Village is a Swedish woman called Molla. Molla has confided to Lucy that, when she had her children, it brought back unresolved emotions about her own mother, who neglected her. As a result, she visited a psychiatrist who told her that she was grieving for the things she never received from her mother as a child.

In hospital, when Lucy asks her mother why she came to visit her, she replies that Lucy's husband called her and asked her to. Lucy falls asleep and, when she wakes up from a nightmare, her mother soothingly urges her to rest. Later, they talk in the dark and Lucy's mother apologises for the humiliation that having so little money caused when she and her siblings were growing up. Lucy is embarrassed, saying it didn't matter and points out that they are all fine now. Her mother contradicts her, however, reminding her that her brother sleeps with pigs and still reads children's books. She also admits that Lucy's sister is still angry with her over being picked on at school. Lucy suggests that it is unfair of Vicky to blame her, but her mother disagrees declaring that it is a mother's job to protect her children. Lucy tells her mother that she still remembers being locked in the truck but her mother doesn't seem to understand what she is talking about. She wants to add that she particularly remembers the time when she was locked in the truck with a long brown snake but she can't bear to say the word.

Back in the sixth grade, Lucy had a social studies teacher called Mr Haley who commanded the respect of all the children. One day, Lucy had to ask Mr Haley for the bathroom pass during class and, when she returned it, one of her classmates made fun of her. Mr. Haley noticed this and angrily told the children that they should never feel that they are better than anyone else. As a result, Lucy fell instantly in love with him. Mr Haley also taught the class about the exploitation of American Indians by the first American settlers. Lucy sympathised with the bravery of Black Hawk and, when she got home, asked her mother if she knew "what we did to the Indians". Her mother replied that she didn't "give a damn". At the end of that year, Mr Haley left the school and, in retrospect, Lucy realised he probably went to Vietnam.

By the third day of her hospital visit, Lucy's mother is starting to look tired and Lucy dreads her leaving. She is then told that her blood tests indicate she needs an urgent CAT scan. In the middle of the night Lucy is taken to the basement of the hospital for the scan, leaving her mother in her room. When she gets there, however, her scan is delayed for some time as the machine breaks down. When Lucy eventually emerges from the room, she finds her mother waiting for her in the dark basement corridor.

The next day, Toothache brings in a gossip magazine and tells Lucy that the results of her scan are fine. Lucy reads out a story from the magazine about a woman in Wisconsin who had her arm chopped off by an escapee from a psychiatric hospital. This all took place as her husband, who had been tied up, helplessly looked on. Lucy comments on how awful the story is but her mother replies that it could have been worse as, on the news, she has seen men who have had to witness their wives being raped. Lucy remembers that as a child she was tempted to run up to complete strangers and ask them to rescue her from the "bad things" going on in her home. When her mother closes her eyes, Lucy feels sad and lonely and goes to the nurses' station to call her family. During the call, Lucy tells her daughters over and over again that she loves them.

Lucy reveals that, in the past few years, she has become fascinated with a particular sculpture in the Metropolitan Museum of Art. The sculpture is of a tortured looking man whose children are staring up into his face and clinging to him. The accompanying placard explains that the man is being starved to death in prison and his children are offering themselves to him "as food". Lucy likes to visit the statue unaccompanied, feeling it speaks only to her.

In hospital, Lucy's mother shows her daughter a photograph of an actress called Annie Appleby in the gossip magazine. She says that Annie's father, Elgin Appleby, used to be friends with Lucy's father. They both try to sum up their impression of Annie Appleby from the photograph. Lucy finally concludes that she "looks like she's seen stuff" and her mother enthusiastically agrees.

Several years after leaving hospital, Lucy's marriage is under strain. She has discovered that William has become close to the family friend who brought the girls to see her in hospital and feels humiliated. After an argument with William, Lucy goes to an art exhibition opening with him without bothering to change her clothes. At the exhibition, Lucy bumps into the artist she had an affair with at college. She immediately realises that he is critically assessing the outfit she is wearing and is suddenly conscious of her lack of style. The incident causes Lucy to reflect that the desire to feel superior to other people is one of the most unpleasant human characteristics.

A few months after Lucy meets her in the clothing store, Lucy discovers that Sarah Payne is making a rare public appearance at a literary debate in New York Public Library. Lucy attends the event where the panel are discussing the nature of fiction and its purpose. During the debate Sarah confirms that she received hate mail after one of her characters referred to a former American president as "a senile old man whose wife ruled the country with her astrology charts." An audience member asks Sarah whether this also expresses her own opinion about the former President. Sarah replies that it is not her job to help readers distinguish between a narrative voice and the opinion of the author. When asked what she believes her job is as a fiction writer, Sarah Payne replies that it is, "to report on the human condition, to tell us who we are and what we think and what we do." At the end of the debate, Lucy hears the man who once criticised the 'compassion' in Sarah's work make a snide remark about the author. She goes home feeling slightly disillusioned with New York. Nevertheless, the experience prompts Lucy to begin writing her own story that night.

In hospital, as they discuss the gossip magazine, Lucy expresses surprise that her mother would care about how famous people felt. She immediately regrets the comment, feeling she has been unkind to her mother and begs her not to leave. Her mother promises that she isn't going anywhere. Lucy tries to hold back her tears as she knows that both her parents loathe "the act of crying." In an effort to prevent it, she painfully squeezes her legs together and, the next day, a bruise has formed on her thigh. When the doctor examines her, he sees the bruise but makes no comment and Lucy is horrified to find herself crying. The doctor puts his hand comfortingly on her forehead and assures Lucy that she will soon be able to return to her daughters. As he leaves, he makes a fist, kisses it and holds it out towards her.

Shortly after the library event, Lucy attends a residential writer's workshop led by Sarah Payne. One day, during a class, a large cat jumps through an open window into the classroom. Both Lucy and Sarah visibly jump with fright and one of the students (a psychoanalyst) asks Sarah how long she has suffered from post-traumatic stress. Sarah continues with the class, stressing the importance of not making judgements about other people in life or in their writing.

Lucy has a private tutorial with Sarah, taking in written versions of the conversations she had with her mother when she was in hospital. Sarah praises Lucy's work and assures her it will be published but also warns her that she will be criticised for "combining poverty and abuse". Sarah points out that Lucy's work is really "about a mother who loves her daughter. Imperfectly." Sarah hugs Lucy who expresses sympathy over the tactless comment the psychoanalyst made about PTSD in class. Sarah expresses her dislike of people who use their professional expertise to make someone feel small in no uncertain terms. After that day, Lucy never sees Sarah again.

In hospital, Lucy and her mother discuss Marilyn Mathews, an older girl who was always kind to Lucy. Lucy's mother reveals that she saw a woman in the public library who bore a strong resemblance to Marilyn and tried to strike up a conversation with her. The woman refused to acknowledge her, however, and the incident made Lucy's mother angry. Lucy sympathetically responds, "Screw 'em," causing her mother to comment on the bad language her daughter has picked up while living in New York. Lucy privately reflects that she overheard all the bad language she knows while living in the garage with her parents. After the incident in the library, Lucy's mother discovered that the real Marilyn Mathews married her childhood sweetheart, Charlie Macauley. The marriage was not a happy one as Charlie went to fight in Vietnam and was never the same when he returned. Lucy's mother predicts that Lucy will get better, although she will have "some problems" in her life. Lucy asks what sort of problems she is referring to and her mother specifies marriage problems.

After Lucy has been living in the Village for a while, she attends her first Gay Pride parade with her family. While she is watching the parade, Lucy becomes upset at the sight of men dressed up in drag as it brings back a traumatic memory from childhood. The memory is of her brother crying as he paraded up Amgash main street wearing women's clothing. Following him, in his truck, was their father, who was screaming homophobic abuse at his son. Later that day, Lucy and her sister went back to the garage where their mother explained that their father had caught his son in the "disgusting" act of trying on women's clothing. That night Lucy saw her father lying next to their brother and rocking him like a baby. Both of them were crying.

Lucy and her mother begin a conversation about Elvis Presley, who Lucy's mother describes as "just a big old piece of trash". Lucy points out that their own family was also "trash" but her mother furiously objects, saying that their ancestors were some of the first settlers in the country. Lucy privately reflects that she would like to hear her mother explain to all the neighbours in Amgash that they cannot be considered trash as their ancestors killed all the American Indians.

Shortly after leaving hospital Lucy meets a woman who becomes a close friend. Lucy's friend also has a difficult relationship with her mother and tells Lucy that they used to hit each other when they fought. Lucy describes this behaviour as "trashy" and her friend admits that her family "were trash." After the event, Lucy feels awful for her thoughtless remark. The incident causes Lucy to remember a time in high school when a teacher gently rebuked her for using the word 'cheap' in an essay.

In hospital, the discussion of Elvis leads Lucy's mother to talk about Mississippi Mary who, like the King, came from Tupelo and was raised in poverty. Lucy's mother says that Mary escaped her humble origins by marrying the captain of the football team at school, whose family had money. Mary went on to have five or six daughters and led a happy life until she discovered that her husband had been having an affair with his secretary for thirteen years. When she found out, she had a heart attack. Lucy's mother reflects that both Mary and Elvis experienced the transition from being very poor to very wealthy but it didn't do either of them any good.

A few years before writing her story, Lucy goes to consult a plastic surgeon, as she has begun to see unwelcome traces of both her mother and her father in her face. The doctor administers some facial injections to make her look like "herself" again. When Lucy goes for a follow-up appointment she observes a young boy curiously watching a very old lady in the waiting room. Lucy is moved when the old lady gets up to leave and the boy opens the door for her.

Lucy thinks about her brother. She remembers a time when she was six years old and came across a group of boys beating up her terrified brother. She also recalls overhearing a conversation between her parents where her father said he couldn't bear it if her brother was sent to Vietnam as the army would kill him. As it turned out, he wasn't called upon to serve in Vietnam but overhearing this conversation made Lucy realise that her father loved her brother. Lucy also remembers a Labor Day when her father took her alone to the Black Hawk Festival. He bought her a candied apple there but Lucy was horrified to find that the crust of the apple was too hard for her to eat. Her father took the apple and ate it himself and, at that moment, Lucy loved her father for not making her feel bad about it.

Back in the hospital, as it gets dark, Lucy tries to coax her mother into admitting that she loves her and they both begin to laugh. Lucy closes her eyes and suggests that her mother can say it while she is not looking. When there is no response, Lucy opens her eyes and her mother says, "When your eyes are closed."

Lucy says that in her writing class, Sarah Payne told her pupils that it is important for a writer to address any weaknesses in their story before the reader does. Lucy confesses that she is afraid that her readers will not understand that her mother was unable to say 'I love you', or her own acceptance of this fact.

The next day, Lucy goes for an x-ray which seems to show a blockage. Her doctor tells her that she may need surgery and Lucy begins to panic. As the doctor reassures her, Lucy's mother stands up and says it is time for her to leave. Lucy begs her to stay but she is adamant and leaves that day. Lucy spends a further five weeks in hospital and misses her mother terribly.

At the time of Lucy's stay in hospital, AIDS had become a serious issue in New York and yellow stickers are stuck on the doors of the hospital rooms containing AIDS patients. One day Lucy is lying on a gurney in a hospital corridor waiting to have more tests. Opposite, she notices a half-open door with a yellow sticker and sees that the man inside the room is staring intently at her. The man maintains his stare and Lucy feels that he is begging her for something.

Lucy's doctor comes to tell her that she doesn't require surgery after all and he apologises for frightening her. Lucy understands that the error stems from the doctor's genuine concern for her, which is further demonstrated when he calls in to check on her every weekend, claiming he has to look in on another patient. During her nine-week stay, the only day the doctor fails to visit is Father's Day. Lucy feels jealous of his children.

Lucy worries about whether her mother returned home safely and is unable to call her as she can only make local or collect calls from the hospital. She remembers once feeling homesick and trying to make a collect call to her parents but her mother refused to accept the charges. With this in mind, she asks William to call her mother. After making the call, William confirms that her mother got home safely but apologetically replies in the negative when Lucy asks if her mother had anything else to say.

Lucy's friend Molla visits her in hospital and, once again, talks about how much she hates her mother. Molla's monologue reminds Lucy of Sarah Payne's belief that each of us has only "one story" to tell.

On one of her husband's rare visits, Lucy wants to spend their time talking but William is tired and lies on the bed with her watching TV. When the doctor comes in, he looks surprised and then comments that it is nice for them to spend some time together. Lucy experiences a "twang" in her head but only appreciates its significance at a later date. Years later, when her daughters are nineteen and twenty, Lucy does have 'trouble' in her marriage, just as her mother predicted, and they both remarry. Lucy reflects that the day William came to the hospital might have been the same day he discovered that he had been left a considerable amount of money by his father: something that Lucy only learned about when she went home. The funds, which William inherited when he was thirty-five, came from his German grandfather's war profiteering. Lucy remembers that when she first met her future mother-in-law, William's mother insisted on buying her some new clothes. Later, when she introduced Lucy to a friend at their wedding, she announced, "Lucy comes from nothing." After leaving hospital, Lucy repeatedly dreams that she and her babies are going to be killed by the Nazis. She never tells her husband about the dream.

Lucy writes to her mother, telling her she loves her and saying she will never forget her visit. Her mother writes back on a postcard showing the Chrysler Building at night. The card reads, "I will never forget either."

When Lucy gets out of hospital she is overjoyed to be reunited with her daughters. Her joy turns to deep sadness, however, when she discovers that Jeremy has died from AIDS. Previously unaware that Jeremy was gay or ill, Lucy begins to wonder if the AIDS patient she saw in the hospital could have been her friend.

Lucy remembers that, even at the Congregational Church they attended, her family were 'outcasts'. Only when they went for their Thanksgiving meal would other members of the congregation be civil to them. Once she is married, she and William go to homeless shelters to serve up food on Thanksgiving until William tells her he can't do it anymore.

Lucy goes back to the doctor for regular check-ups after she leaves hospital. One day, however, she learns that he has retired when she is called in for an appointment with a new doctor. Lucy never sees him again.

At Sarah Payne's writing workshop, one of the students tells Sarah that she admires her work, particularly the parts about New Hampshire. The student goes on to talk about Janie Templeton, a friend from New Hampshire, whose father had a breakdown and would walk around the house masturbating. Lucy is shaken by this story as it is the first time she has heard of 'the Thing' happening in other households. Sarah notices that Lucy has found the story distressing and briskly dismisses the student. The next day, in class, Sarah Payne makes a speech about the need to go "to the page with a heart as open as the heart of God".

After the publication of her first novel, Lucy goes to see a female doctor. Before the appointment, Lucy writes down all the things she feels she cannot say, including the story of Janie Templeton's father, the things that went on in her childhood home and the things that happened in her marriage. The doctor reads what she has written, thanks Lucy and tells her it will be ok.

After her mother's hospital visit, Lucy doesn't travel to see her family for another nine years: partly because she is busy with her daughters and writing and partly because they seem awkward and resentful when she calls. When she finally sees her mother again, it is to visit her at a Chicago hospital where she is dying. Lucy wants to reciprocate the support her mother gave her when she was in hospital but, on the second night, her mother says she needs her to leave. Lucy reluctantly agrees and tells her mother that she will miss her. Her mother agrees and, as Lucy leaves the room, she shouts, "Mommy I love you." For a moment she waits outside listening for an answer but there is none. Lucy explains to her father what her mother has asked of her and begs him to let her know when the funeral service will be. He is adamant that there will be no service and is true to his word.

A year later, Lucy travels to her family home in Amgash to see her father, who is dying from pneumonia. At his bedside she repeatedly tells him that she is sorry. In response, her father squeezes her hand and says she has always been, "a good girl". He dies shortly afterwards and, in accordance with his wishes, there is no funeral service.

When Lucy returns to New York, her husband seems like a "stranger" and her children are absorbed in their own lives, leaving Lucy feeling rootless. She realises that, although she comes from a dysfunctional family, she also shares an irrevocable bond with her parents and siblings.

After the publication of Lucy's first novel, which receives good reviews, she has to embark on publicity tours and finds the experience less frightening than expected. She receives many appreciative letters from readers, including one from her former lover, the artist. Lucy replies to all of her letters except this one.

When her daughters leave for college, Lucy is so heartbroken she feels as if she will die. It is at this point that her marriage ends. Lucy refuses to accept alimony from William as she is earning enough in her own right, and is also conscious that his money comes from German war profiteering.

Lucy recalls how, when she first married William at the age of twenty, she tried to become the perfect housewife by buying a recipe book. One day, as she fried some garlic, William had to gently point out that she was cooking an entire bulb rather than a clove and that it should be peeled first. She stopped trying to cook when she had her daughters. Lucy reveals that her new husband, who is a professional cello player, grew up in great poverty with a mother who was in and out of psychiatric care. She has never felt the need to try to impress him in the kitchen.

Lucy remembers that, in the early years of their marriage, William often took her to Yankee games. She loved watching the games, particularly as the sun set over the Bronx. While many memories of her first marriage now make Lucy sad, she can still recall the Yankee games with complete happiness.

After the death of her parents, Lucy calls her brother once a week but still knows very little about him. She knows he lives in the family house and works on farm machinery but has no idea if he has a girlfriend or boyfriend. Lucy also regularly speaks to her sister, who is always ranting about her husband's selfish habits and their lack of money. Lucy regularly gives her sister money for items she says she needs for the children, even when one of them is yoga lessons. Lucy believes her sister feels she is owed the money and thinks she may be right.

In college, Lucy shared a room with a girl who felt neglected by her mother. One day, out of the blue, the girl's mother sent her daughter a package of cheese. Neither Lucy nor the girl liked cheese but Lucy's roommate couldn't bear to throw it away and decided to keep it on their outside window ledge. After several months, Lucy's roommate asked her to dispose of the cheese while she was in class.

Lucy admits that, despite her earlier feelings about the artist's shirt, she and her daughters have been frequenting Bloomingdale's for years. There were a number of years, however, when her daughters would not go with her as they were furious with her for leaving their father. In all the apartments Lucy has had since the divorce she has ensured that there was a guest bedroom for her daughters. The fact that they have never stayed over breaks Lucy's heart. William is now married to the 'family friend' who brought the girls to see her in hospital. When her daughters refer to their 'stepmother' Lucy has to fight the temptation to point out that the woman never washed their faces or brushed their hair while she was in hospital.

One day, Lucy and Becka see the destruction of the World Trade Center on TV together. As Becka watches the second plane hit the second Twin Tower she looks stricken and cries out "Mommy". Sometimes, when she is alone, Lucy echoes this cry without knowing if she is thinking of Becka, or calling out for her own mother. Lucy's other daughter, Chrissy, recently told her that she loves the new partners of both her parents but hopes that they both die so that Lucy and William will get back together. Lucy is very aware of the hurt she has caused her children and knows only too well that we carry our childhood wounds with us for the rest of our lives.

Lucy still sometimes thinks about Sarah Payne, although she doesn't know where she is living and Sarah hasn't written any more books. She reflects that she never discovered what Sarah's 'one story' was. Lucy, on the other hand, finally feels she is able to declare her identity and story with confidence.

Lucy thinks about the beautiful effects of the setting sun on the farmland around her childhood home and reflects that life still "amazes" her.

# STYLE

*Lucy Barton* is a short novel made up of multiple short chapters or extracts. The story is told through Lucy's first person narrative in a scattered form. This reflects the fact that Lucy recounts her memories as they arise in her train of thought without attempting to arrange them chronologically.

Lucy's narrative voice has a confessional and autobiographical feel which is achieved through several techniques. One of the most striking is the tentative quality of Lucy's voice reflecting her recognition that, although she wants her account to be as truthful as possible, her memory may not be entirely accurate. This is conveyed through little qualifying phrases such as, "At least I remember it that way" and "But maybe that wasn't what my mother said." By using these telling asides, Lucy demonstrates her realisation that memory can place a subjective spin on events.

Another unusual characteristic of Lucy's voice is her tendency to repeat or clarify something she has already said. This propensity towards repetition reveals her desire to tell her story in a way that leaves no room for misunderstandings on the part of the reader. It also lends an urgency to Lucy's story, making it feel more like a conversation (in which unconscious verbal repetitions are common) rather than a written account.

The conversational tone of Lucy's narrative and its lack of chronological order mean that the reader's relationship with Lucy is like a growing friendship. Just as, in life, intimacies are built upon gradually revealing more of yourself to another person, the reader comes to understand Lucy by fitting all the fragmented stories of her life together to form a whole. To emphasise this effect, just as even close friends will withhold certain aspects of their lives, Lucy circles around particularly traumatic events in her life, or simply leaves them out altogether. This leaves the reader to analyse the connections between Lucy's stories and make an informed guess at filling in the blanks.

Another narrative quirk of Lucy's is her decision to leave many of her characters unnamed. The reader never finds out the real names of the doctor; the family friend; the artist; Lucy's brother or even her parents. This gives the narrative an almost mythic feel, as if these characters are archetypes. Lucy doesn't reveal the full names of these characters as, for her purposes, the reader does not need to know them. As she emphasises at the end of the novel, this is her story alone and the names she gives the other characters reflects the ways she thinks of them in her head.

In terms of genre, Lucy Barton isn't easy to neatly categorise but perhaps best falls under the label of domestic literary fiction. Strout's interest is in character rather than plot and, while some of the incidents that Lucy relates are shocking (such as her brother's public humiliation by her father and her own experiences in the truck), many appear, at least on the surface, to be humdrum. There are no car chases, no cliff-hangers, just conversations and descriptions of largely unremarkable incidents. This is where the power of the novel lies, however, as Strout's ability to capture the natural tone of ordinary conversations is totally credible, giving her writing its authentic and truthful tone. Meanwhile, her portrayal of everyday events and encounters illustrates how it is the accumulation of such moments that makes up a life. When Lucy asks, "How do we find out what the daily fabric of a life was?" she echoes the very purpose of Strout's novel: to convey the 'daily fabric' of the life of her protagonist. In less skilled hands, Strout's subject matter could easily be dull but her acute sensitivity to what makes us human transforms an ordinary life into compelling and profound subject matter. As Hilary Mantel said in her praise of *Lucy Barton*, "Writing of this quality comes from a commitment to listening, from a perfect attunement to the human condition, from an attention to reality so exact that it goes beyond a skill and becomes a virtue."

# THEMES & IMAGERY

## THEMES

### Identity

While praising *My Name is Lucy Barton* for its content, at least one critic has criticised Strout for her novel's apparently unimaginative and slightly archaic-sounding title. Although the critics may have a point, Strout's choice of title deliberately emphasises the central theme of the novel - female identity. Directly referencing Lucy's confident assertion of who she is at the end of the novel, the title reflects the protagonist's journey towards becoming herself.

When Lucy first meets Sarah Payne, one of the most significant things she notices is that the other woman is still hesitant in telling people her name. Lucy completely empathises with this lack of self-confidence as, at this point in the narrative, she feels just as hesitant about her own identity.

Through Lucy's accounts of her childhood, the reader begins to understand the way that her sense of identity has been undermined from an early age. While living in the garage, she has little sense even of what she looks like, as the only mirror the family possess is hung too high for her. Socially isolated, the only sense of identity that she gains from her classmates is the knowledge that she is dirty and smelly. Lucy's poor self-image is then exacerbated when she hits puberty and begins to develop breasts, causing her mother to comment that she is, "starting to look like one of the cows in the Pedersons' barn". The only thing that Lucy knows for sure about herself at this point is that she wants to be a writer. It is only this ambition that provides her with a sense of who she is.

Due to the suffocating limitations of her childhood, Lucy's journey towards a sense of identity only really begins when she leaves home. At college she not only gains academic knowledge, but also learns about the aspects of the world she has missed out on from her peers. When she is first married to William, however, Lucy is still unsure of who she is and feels she should try to become the perfect housewife (humorously illustrated in her anecdote about attempting to fry an unpeeled garlic bulb). Although she continues to believe that she is a writer, she lacks the confidence to declare this to others. Even with the first publication of one of her stories, she diminishes her achievement in front of Jeremy and her mother, describing her stories as "dumb".

Lucy's difficulty in taking full ownership of her identity is also hampered by her mother's refusal to listen to any details about her life, or acknowledge who her daughter has become. The string of hard-luck stories her mother tells about women from their hometown, however, makes it clear that this is the kind of female identity Lucy has escaped.

While the stories told by Lucy's mother focus on women whose lives have fallen apart due to the absence of men, Lucy goes on to prove that her own sense of identity is autonomous from her husband's. In fact, her decision to leave William is partly based upon her belief that she cannot be truly herself within the marriage. The realisation that she must be true to herself (despite her guilt about breaking up the family unit) and write novels that come from her heart finally allows her to exceed the achievements of her mentor, Sarah Payne. Her emphatic declaration of who she is towards the end of the novel is a testament to just how far she has travelled in her voyage of self-discovery.

## **Mother/daughter relationships**

Elizabeth Strout believes the relationship between mother and child to be "the most primal relationship we can have" and in this novel she focuses on the complexity of mother-daughter relationships. It is the arrival of Lucy's mother at her hospital bedside and the symbolic significance of that visit for her daughter that stands at the heart of the story. Although Lucy hasn't seen her mother for many years, however, Strout does not deliver the schmaltzy, sentimental reunion we might expect. While it is undoubtedly maternal love that drives Lucy's mother to visit her daughter, their relationship remains a difficult one.

The strong maternal instinct of Lucy's mother is proven by her journey to New York and her constant five-day vigil by her daughter's bedside. Her love is also demonstrated in numerous small gestures, such as the way she calls Lucy 'Wizzle' and squeezes her foot through the sheets to reassure her. Almost every gesture of love, however, is counterbalanced by an incident where she deliberately withholds herself from her daughter. When Lucy asks her mother why she came to visit, instead of saying what Lucy wants to hear, she matter-of-factly replies that Lucy's husband asked her to. In doing so, she detracts from the emotion behind the act. Similarly, after bonding with her daughter over stories of their hometown, Lucy's mother then destroys their sense of intimacy by refusing to hear anything about Lucy's life in New York. Most strikingly of all, despite her daughter's playful coaxing, she is unable to tell Lucy that she loves her.

Lucy's joyful cry of "Mommy" when she first sees her mother is an instinctive, childlike response. Able to sleep through the night for the first time, Lucy draws comfort simply from her mother's presence. She also takes great joy in their seemingly mundane conversations and, despite her mother's often hurtful behaviour, takes an appeasing role.

Lucy's need for signs of love from her mother is palpable, even in adulthood, and her attempt to coax her mother into declaring her love is profoundly moving. This moment sums up the poignant tug-of-war dynamic of their relationship. Constantly aware that her daughter wants more from her than she is prepared to give, Lucy's mother pulls away each time Lucy attempts to draw her closer.

Despite their difficulties in communicating with each other, there are also moments of real connection between the two women in the novel. Although Lucy and her mother are very different, there are also moments when Strout emphasises similarities in their speech patterns and mannerisms. This is nicely illustrated in the moment when they study the photograph of Annie Appleby in a magazine and, after much consideration, both conclude that she "looks like she's seen stuff". Later in the novel, Lucy comes to realise that she not only shares some of her mother's thought processes but has also come to look like her, prompting her to visit "the doctor women go to when they don't want to look like their mothers". In this way, Strout emphasises not only the bonds of love and shared history between mother and daughter but the indelible genetic link.

Lucy is not the only character in the novel whose conflicted relationship with her mother continues into adulthood. Like Lucy, her roommate at college felt neglected as a child and is therefore unable to part with a package of cheese her mother unexpectedly sends to her. Lucy completely understands her roommate's interpretation of the cheese as a token of love and eventually helps her to painlessly dispose of it. Meanwhile, Lucy's friend, Molla, claims to have been neglected by her mother as a child and, as a result, has to face unresolved emotions when she has children of her own.

In her interactions with her own daughters, Lucy tries to compensate for what was lacking in her relationship with her mother, frequently telling them that she loves them. In contrast to her parents, who made it clear that they despised tears, she kisses and comforts her girls when they cry. Having known the humiliation of being poor and dirty, she is also distressed when the 'family friend' brings her daughters to the hospital with dirty faces and tangled hair.

Despite the love she lavishes on her daughters, Lucy's relationship with them is irreparably damaged when she leaves their father. For a number of years, Christina and Becka are furious with her for fracturing their family and, although they eventually soften towards their mother, never regain the same level of intimacy. This is made clear in Lucy's dismay that neither of her daughters ever stay overnight with her, even though she keeps a spare room specifically for that purpose. The situation she finds herself in makes Lucy think of Kathie Nicely who became estranged from her family after leaving her husband for another man. Lucy feels great guilt at the pain she has caused her daughters. She is also aware, however, that if she had stayed in her first marriage (as her own mother did) her growth as a writer and a human being would have been stunted. Although she would do almost anything for her daughters, the one thing she is unable to completely sacrifice to them is her identity.

## The Nature of Love

When Sarah Payne reads Lucy's story she suggests that it reflects the way, "we all love imperfectly". The notion of imperfect love is best embodied in Lucy's mother who loves her daughter but is unable to express it. It is also illustrated in the way Lucy feels about her siblings as, although they have never been close, she is aware of a strong, invisible bond between them.

One of the tragedies of Lucy's life is that she goes through much of it feeling unloved. Despite this, she is a character who exudes love for others. Lucy's unconditional love for her mother and her daughters is a palpable force. She also frequently declares that she loves people she knows less well (her doctor, her neighbour, her nurse). While these declarations might seem flippant from the mouth of another character, Strout makes it clear that Lucy is completely sincere. Lucy's ready attachment to relative strangers is an expression of her love for humanity in general. It also extends to a love of the world and life itself. Despite the pain she has suffered, Lucy's openness to love in all its forms proves to be her salvation.

## Self-expression

Closely related to the imperfect nature of love is Strout's interest in the difficulties of self-expression. A great deal of the novel concerns the emotions that bubble beneath the surface of everything we say and do but are never fully expressed.

Lucy's relationship with her Jewish doctor is a prime example of this. Although they say little of any significance to each other, Lucy conveys an unspoken connection between them which seems to be based on a mutual recognition that the other person has suffered in some significant way. Through small, compassionate gestures the doctor conveys his concern for Lucy's welfare and the understanding that her suffering is not purely physical. The undercurrent of emotion that he cannot fully express is beautifully illustrated in the moment when he kisses his fist and holds it in the air as he leaves her room. This strange, awkward gesture is the doctor's best attempt at expressing his love and concern for his patient without overstepping professional boundaries.

At a more extreme level, Lucy's mother epitomises the

difficulties of self-expression. While her sole reason for visiting Lucy in hospital is to show her love for her, she is never able to verbally express this and, in fact, often gives the opposite impression. Unable to say 'I love you', or to discuss anything remotely personal, she talks only about the misfortunes of others. Underlying her mundane conversation, however, is an urgency of tone, packed with all the emotion of the things she is unable to say. Like the doctor, she also often expresses deep emotion through gestures, wiggling her fingers or squeezing her daughter's foot.

Although Lucy is much more expressive of her emotions than her mother, there is also a great deal that she feels she cannot say, either through fear of upsetting her mother or because the subject is simply too painful to talk about. The way Lucy imposes silence upon herself to appease her mother is illustrated in the scene where she desperately tries not to cry in front of her. Remembering that her parents always abhorred crying, she distracts herself by painfully squeezing her legs together. When a bruise forms the next day, it is a visible symbol of the pain created by repressed emotions.

For Lucy, writing becomes an important form of self-expression, allowing her to explore experiences that she feels unable to discuss with others. Even in her narrative, however, she admits that there are some things she cannot say about her childhood and the break-up of her marriage. It is these experiences that she eventually writes down for the eyes of her therapist only.

## **The pain of childhood**

Lucy says that whenever she hears a child desperately sobbing, she thinks, "it is one of the truest sounds a child can make." This statement sums up the unsentimental and unflinchingly honest portrayal of childhood in the novel. In *Lucy Barton*, Strout debunks the romanticised concept of childhood as a carefree period in our lives by repeatedly reminding the reader of how intensely unhappy children are capable of being.

Through Lucy's childhood memories in particular, the author powerfully evokes the raw intensity of emotion experienced by children during their formative years – from loneliness, to humiliation, to fear. Lucy's is, of course, more traumatic than the average childhood, involving poverty; social humiliation and isolation; and the dread of being locked in her father's truck – and these are just the incidents she can bear to reveal. Although readers can only guess at the incidents Lucy cannot articulate, the horror of them is conveyed in her childhood urge to run up to strangers and beg them to save her from the "bad things" going on in her home.

Throughout the novel Strout illustrates how the pain we experience as children is carried into later life and shapes the adults we become. The effect of Lucy's childhood neglect is still painfully evident, from her desperation for proof of her mother's love to her longstanding phobia of snakes. Meanwhile, the insomnia suffered by Lucy's mother is a legacy from her own childhood, as she never felt safe enough to go to sleep at night. Similarly, Sarah Payne unconsciously reveals that she suffers from her own childhood demons in her extreme reaction to a cat jumping through the window during a writing workshop.

Lucy is eager to protect her own daughters from pain but, nevertheless, inflicts it upon them when she divorces their father. Although by this time they are young adults, Becka and Christina are deeply hurt by the divorce as they retain childlike feelings about their parents. This is demonstrated when Christina reveals that, even though she has become fond of the new partners of both her parents, there is part of her that hopes that they die so that Lucy and William will get back together again. Lucy understands only too well how deeply her actions have hurt her daughters and suffers great guilt. As a result, the trauma she suffered as a child and the pain she has inflicted on her own daughters become inextricably linked. When she finds herself crying out "Mommy", she is calling out for her own mother and, at the same time, echoing the cry of Becka when she watched the destruction of the World Trade Center. In this moment she represents the hurt child lurking within every adult.

## **Kindness**

Kindness is a quality that Lucy greatly appreciates in other people. She mourns the fact that the famous declaration of Blanche DuBois in *Gone with the Wind* ("I have always depended on the kindness of strangers") has become a cliché as she considers it "a beautiful and true line". Many of Lucy's memories involve demonstrations of kindness on the part of strangers or relative strangers: the janitor who lets her into a heated classroom after school; the teacher who defends her against bullying; the boy who opens the door for an old lady in the doctor's surgery and the TLC provided by the Jewish doctor in hospital. Lucy holds on to these positive memories of man's capacity for kindness as an antidote to the instances of cruelty and unkindness she has experienced during her life.

## **Loneliness**

One of the things that Lucy is deprived of when she is a child is the company of others. The lonely location of their home on the outskirts of town reflects the family's social status. Treated as pariahs, they have only one another. Instead of bringing them closer, however, the situation causes each family member to turn in upon themselves and live within a bubble of isolation. Lucy's earliest memories are tinged with loneliness, leading her to befriend a solitary tree, and it is a sensation that haunts her for the rest of her life. It is also the emotion that prompts her to want to become a writer. When Lucy reads a book about Tilly, a girl who is scorned by other children for her dirtiness and poverty, she feels less alone in the world and sees writing as a way of alleviating the loneliness of others.

Lucy loves New York because, in contrast to her rural hometown, it offers many opportunities to meet strangers. Whenever she finds herself dwelling on the loneliness of her childhood, Lucy seeks out company in the city by striking up conversations with strangers. Even within a bustling city like New York, however, the novel presents images of loneliness: Lucy's sense of isolation in her private hospital room, the old lady who cries out for help from her hospital bed with little response, and the quarantined AIDs patient who sits alone in his room as he faces death.

## **Mortality**

Closely related to the novel's exploration of loneliness is the theme of mortality and the inevitability of human suffering. Death, or the fear of it, is a constant lurking presence in the novel, from Lucy's fear of dying in hospital to the AIDS epidemic and the depiction of

9/11.

Lucy encounters a number of dying people during her story: the old lady in the hospital bed next to her own; the quarantined AIDs patient (who may or may not be her friend, Jeremy); her mother, and her father. Each encounter impacts on her in a different way. Hearing the old woman's cries, which go largely ignored by the hospital staff, prompts her to later beg the nurses caring for her own dying mother not to let her suffer. Although the nurses try to reassure her, Lucy reads in their eyes, "the deepest fatigue of people who cannot do any more about anything." When Lucy observes the AIDS patient staring at her from the isolation of his hospital room, the moment recalls an earlier incident where Lucy misguidedly confesses to Jeremy that she almost envies gay men with AIDS, "because they have each other". The patient's burning gaze seems to demand that Lucy bears witness to his final moments in which he is isolated and utterly alone. Most poignant of all these experiences is the moment when Lucy's dying mother asks her daughter to leave. While Lucy wants to be there for her mother, the request is an acknowledgement that, in the moment of death, we are all alone. Her wish to spare Lucy the sight of her suffering is a last gift of love to her daughter.

### **Poverty & Class**

As a child, Lucy experiences the extremes of poverty. Living in a relative's garage until she is eleven years old, she is frequently "ravenous", cold and dirty. Through the shocking details of Lucy's account, Strout provides an uncomfortable reminder that social deprivation is not confined to underdeveloped countries. She also brings home the stigma and shame experienced by those suffering from poverty. The lowly economic status of Lucy's family literally places them outside of society, making them pariahs. While classmates tell Lucy and her sister that they "stink", a second-grade teacher humiliates Vicky by announcing that poverty is no excuse for being dirty.

Lucy's siblings remain mired in the poverty they grew up in for the rest of their lives. In Lucy's case, however, poverty acts as a stimulus to escape her origins. Her academic success is partly the result of staying late at school to keep warm, while her desire to be a writer is inspired after reading a book about a girl named Tilly who, like her, is "dirty and poor".

Although Lucy successfully makes the transition from poor little girl to an upper middle-class woman who shops in Bloomingdale's, she is never able to escape her origins entirely. Acutely conscious of her background, she feels inferior to the other students at university. As a result, she falls in love with 'the artist': an arrogant professor who further undermines her self-esteem by criticising her thrift store style. Significantly, while Lucy is prepared to sacrifice having children in order to stay with the artist, she finally breaks it off with him after he makes a particularly insensitive remark about her childhood. After Lucy reveals to him that her family were extremely poor and lived mainly on baked beans, the artist makes a crass joke about farting. It is the flippant nature of his comment that makes Lucy realise he will never be able to grasp the nature of her experience.

Even after she marries and moves to New York, Lucy experiences a loneliness which largely stems from her class origins. Aware that she wouldn't be able to explain her childhood to her middle-class, New York friends, she feels isolated by the things she is unable to say. Her first husband, William, is far more sympathetic than the artist and Lucy initially feels that he is able to grasp the awful nature of her childhood. As the marriage progresses, however, Lucy becomes increasingly conscious of the chasm between William's comfortable middle-class experiences and her own. While William does his best to bridge the gap, Lucy can never truly believe that she is worthy of him, creating a further distance between them. Significantly, her second marriage is to a man who experienced poverty equal to her own as a child.

Through Lucy's account, class prejudice emerges as one on methods through which "we find ways to feel superior to another person, another group of people." It also becomes clear that this kind of prejudice is not restricted to the middle-classes and above. When Lucy's mother denounces Elvis Presley as "trash" and suggests that he only appeals to "cheap" people, she displays the all-too-human urge to assert her own superiority of class and taste. Lucy takes her mother to task on her comment, pointing out that their family was also considered "trash" but then confesses in her narrative that, in a moment of thoughtlessness, she also once described a friend's behaviour as "trashy". While Lucy bitterly regrets her words, her confession reveals that not even she is immune from making class-based judgemental comments.

## **Abuse**

In addition to the miseries of poverty, Lucy suffers abuse in her childhood, the details of which she largely omits from her narrative. The snippets she chooses to reveal, however (indiscriminate beatings, long episodes locked in her father's truck, and her brother's public humiliation in women's clothing), are serious enough for the reader to speculate in horror at what she might have left out.

Lucy's narrative suggests that her father's episodes of aggression and extreme anxiety (referred to as 'the Thing') lie at the heart of the abuse she is unable to put into words. She also hints that her father's behaviour bore some similarity to that of Janie Templeton's father, who also suffered from PTSD and went around the house masturbating. When it comes to beatings, however, Lucy significantly reveals that it was largely her mother who hit her, usually in the presence of her father. This suggests that Lucy's father was in some way the stimulus for the violence and may indicate a cycle of abuse in which the beaten wife then beats her children. There are also suggestions that Lucy's mother was also abused as a child when she reveals to her daughter that she learned to cat nap as she was too scared to sleep at night.

As well as childhood abuse, Strout highlights a number of other ways in which power tends to be abused in society. Lucy, who has a natural affinity with the underdog, comments on her dislike of the human urge to exert a sense of superiority by making others feel inferior. When, in high school, Mr Haley teaches her class about the exploitation of American Indians by the first American settlers, Lucy is outraged and later asks her mother if she knows "what we did to the Indians". When she replies that she doesn't "give a damn" about the Indians, Lucy's mother demonstrates a common human failing. Although she knows what it is like to be unfairly persecuted and socially ostracised on the basis of social class, Lucy's mother is unable to feel sympathy for the American Indians. Instead, she places herself above them in the social hierarchy, proudly telling Lucy that their ancestors were some of the first settlers in the country. This, again, shows a cycle of abuse in which each person attempts to feel better about their own circumstances by asserting their superiority over someone else.

## Nazi Germany

Closely related to Strout's exploration of the abuse of power is her theme of Nazi Germany. For a contemporary novel, there are a surprising number of references to World War II and the Nazis. Lucy's first husband, William, is the son of a German prisoner-of-war who settled in the United States. His ancestry leads to an uncomfortable confrontation with Lucy's father, who killed two innocent German youths during the war. Lucy discovers that her Jewish doctor lost his grandparents and aunts in the Nazi concentration camps and, after leaving hospital, she repeatedly dreams that she and her babies are going to be killed by the Nazis. Finally, the yellow stickers placed on the hospital doors of AIDS patients remind Lucy of the yellow stars worn by Jews during Hitler's regime.

These recurring reminders of Nazi ideology reflect Strout's interest in the way societies maintain systems of power by creating social outcasts. While Hitler's 'social cleansing' is an extreme example of this human propensity, the parallels the narrative draws between Nazism and the demonising of other social groups (the poor, homosexuals etc.) highlight troubling similarities. Lucy's decision not to accept any of the money that William inherits (made largely by his German grandfather from war profiteering) is a symbol of her complete opposition to social abuse.

## PTSD

Post-Traumatic Stress Disorder is another theme that occurs surprisingly frequently in a novel that isn't primarily about war. Lucy's father suffers from PTSD after WWII, as does Janie Templeton's father. The childhood sweetheart of Marilyn Mathews, Charlie Macauley, returns a broken man after fighting in Vietnam. When a cat unexpectedly jumps through the window during a writing workshop it becomes clear that Lucy and Sarah Payne are also fellow-sufferers of PTSD.

The recurrence of PTSD in the novel is, in the majority of these cases, a reminder of the devastating psychological impact that wartime violence has upon its witnesses and perpetrators. It also traces the reverberations that trauma has upon family and loved ones. In the cases of Lucy and Sarah Payne, however, PTSD is also a reminder that personal trauma can take many different forms and that a surprising number of people carry the burden of past traumas around in everyday life.

## Memory

Some time after his death, Lucy learns that her father was haunted by memory. When her brother reveals that their father shot two German boys during WWII and felt guilty about it for the rest of his life, Lucy finally understands his hostile treatment of her first husband. While Lucy's father spends his life unable to escape his memories, for his daughter, memory has a more elusive quality.

Lucy's narrative is driven by memories, all sparked by her mother's five-day hospital visit. Her narrative voice is often hesitant, however, reflecting the fact that she is sometimes uncertain whether her memories are the product of wishful thinking or hindsight. As a result, her account is punctuated by little asides such as, "At least I remember it that way" and "maybe that wasn't what my mother said." Similarly, when Lucy describes her dying father squeezing her hand and saying she has always been "a good girl", she adds, "I am quite certain he said this to me," as if to reassure herself that the incident really happened. Lucy realises that, despite her desire to write an absolutely truthful account, the vagaries of memory may make this impossible.

In the case of Lucy's mother, Strout presents a character who uses selective memory as a strategy to cope with painful experiences. Unlike her husband, who was tormented by memory until he died, Lucy's mother appears to be able to choose what she remembers. Although Lucy finds it hard to believe that her mother could have forgotten about the episodes when she was locked in the truck, her denial of any memory of it seems genuine. Her skill in filtering memories is also demonstrated in the moment when she disapprovingly notes that Lucy has picked up bad language while living in New York, apparently forgetting the obscenities she must have heard at home as a child. Lucy reflects that she will never know what her mother really remembered but it is clear that many of the memories she chooses to forget are moments when she feels she failed her children as a mother. Whether she is even conscious of filtering out these memories is never clear.

## Storytelling

Sarah Payne tells her class of aspiring writers that, "We only have one story". At the heart of *My Name is Lucy Barton* is Lucy's attempt to tell the reader her 'one story' as honestly as possible. Within Lucy's narrative, however, are also the stories of women from her hometown, told to her by her mother, almost as if they are fables or symbolic fairy tales.

The importance of storytelling is crucial to the novel and something that Lucy gradually learns to appreciate as she becomes more confident about who she is. Lucy initially describes the fiction she writes as "dumb" to other people. An important part of her development is to realise how important it is that women's stories should be told – from her own account to the stories of ordinary women whose histories tend to be overlooked, such as Kathie Nicely and Mississippi Mary. Through the stories of Lucy and her mother, Strout emphasises the therapeutic nature of storytelling and its power to bring people together.

## Truth in Art

Closely related to the theme of storytelling is Strout's exploration of truth in art. One of Sarah Payne's aims as a writer is to depict human experience as truthfully as possible and it is a lesson that Lucy strongly adheres to in her own fiction. One of the reasons for Lucy's success as a writer seems to be that she pours the truths she cannot express in her life onto the page.

The ability of art to speak to us as individuals is a theme that recurs throughout the novel. Lucy is initially inspired to become a writer by a book she reads as a child about a poor girl called Tilly. The book resonates with Lucy because it is the first representation she ever reads of a character similar to herself and reading it makes her feel "less alone". In later life, she is also greatly moved by a statue she sees depicting a starving man with his children. The statue touches her deeply as the desperate love she sees in the children's upturned faces reminds Lucy of her own feelings for her mother. As Lucy's response to it feels so personal, she is affronted at the idea of many other people viewing it in a special exhibition.

Throughout the novel, Strout also highlights that the appreciation of art is a very personal experience and what speaks to one person might not speak to another. Lucy, for example, admires the modern art displayed by 'the artist' and her neighbour, Jeremy, but she feels she doesn't understand it. Similarly, when Lucy gives a copy of her favourite childhood book to her daughter, Christina rather harshly describes it as "dumb", as she cannot relate to the story. Through sharing the reading tastes of Lucy's brother, Strout also makes the point that different people look for different things from their experience of art. While Lucy wanted to read about characters like herself in order to feel less lonely, her brother looks for complete escapism in his reading matter. Continuing to read 'The Little House on the Prairie' books well into adulthood, he takes comfort in the stories about a nice family with loving parents, so different from his own.

# IMAGERY

### The Chrysler Building

From Lucy's hospital room there is a view of the Chrysler Building which is particularly impressive when illuminated at night. For Lucy, the shining Chrysler Building reminds her of her love of New York: the city that she longs to be a part of lies just outside her window, but is also tantalising out of reach. On a more general level, its looming presence also represents Lucy's love of life and the beauty she finds in the world. When Lucy's mother sends her a postcard of the Chrysler Building at night it demonstrates that she somehow understands the symbolic importance of the building to her daughter.

### The Single Tree

When Lucy is a girl, she counts her only friend as a single tree that grows in the middle of a cornfield near her home. On one level, Lucy's identification with the isolated tree is a heart-breaking symbol of her loneliness. On another, however, it illustrates Lucy's sensitivity to the beauty of the world and her ability to find hope in her surroundings - no matter how bleak.

The image of the tree is echoed later in the novel when Lucy's mother compares the son of her cousin, Abel Blaine, to a tree that grows and flourishes in the middle of nowhere. Like the tree and Abel, Lucy also goes on to stand alone and flourish despite the barren circumstances of her upbringing.

## **The Starving Father**

In the Metropolitan Museum of Art, Lucy becomes fascinated by a particular sculpture. The piece in question is of a tortured looking man whose children are staring up into his face and clinging to him. The accompanying placard explains that the man is starving to death in prison and his children are offering themselves to him "as food".

Lucy likes to visit the statue furtively and is affronted when she learns that it has been moved to a special exhibition, as she feels the piece speaks personally to her. The stance of the children in the statue and their upturned faces strike a strong chord with Lucy because she feels that the sculptor understood the overwhelming sense of need that children feel for their parents. This echoes her own feeling of need for her mother, which is never fully satisfied.

Although Strout doesn't identify the statue in the novel, she is presumably referring to the real-life masterpiece, 'Ugolino and his Sons' by Jean-Baptiste Carpeaux. The statue illustrates a scene from Dante's *Divine Comedy* in which Ugolino della Gherardesca, a 13th century Italian nobleman, is imprisoned and condemned to die of starvation along with his children. In Dante's text, Ugolino's children entreat their father to eat their bodies in order to end his suffering.

# CHARACTERS

## Lucy Barton

Lucy is the eponymous heroine of her own story and it is the quality of her first person narrative voice that makes Strout's novel so extraordinary. In her narrative, Lucy takes one incident (her nine-week stay in hospital) and uses it as a springboard to recount other significant moments in her life: from her childhood to the failure of her marriage and her development as a writer. The tone of Lucy's voice is gentle, vulnerable and insightful. By putting together the fragmented stories of her life (and sometimes guessing at the ones she feels unable to tell) the reader's relationship with Lucy feels like a deepening friendship.

Central to Lucy's account is her mother's unexpected appearance at her hospital bedside. While, for most of us, a visit from our mother would be nothing out of the ordinary in these circumstances, for Lucy the incident is worthy subject matter for a novel. Having never felt that the mother who hit her "impulsively and vigorously" as a child really loved her, Lucy is astonished that she would have taken the huge step of travelling from Illinois to New York just to see her. As soon as she lays eyes on her mother, Lucy calls her "Mommy" and slips into a childlike role, taking great joy in the simple, gossipy conversations they have.

Underlying Lucy's pleasure in her mother's company is her overwhelming need for love from her, which remains just as strong even in adulthood. Although she experiences moments of anger with her mother, particularly when she claims not to remember certain things about her childhood, Lucy represses these feelings in a desire to please. While she tries to convince herself that her mother's presence should be enough, Lucy still craves confirmation of her affection. This results in the heart-breaking moment when she urges her mother to tell her she loves her. Although she tells the reader that it is 'all right' that her mother cannot say the words, her assurance is unconvincing, particularly as she repeatedly makes a point of telling her own daughters how much she loves them. While Lucy accepts that her mother is incapable of expressing her feelings, it clearly hurts her deeply.

Her mother's visit triggers Lucy to recount stories of other people who have profoundly influenced her life in some way. One of Lucy's most endearing qualities is her love and admiration for people who have shown her kindness: the doctor; her high school teacher; her neighbour; an older girl from school, etc. Lucy thrives on those rare moments of real connection with other people and these incidents have a special place in her heart. She also recounts moments when others have hurt her: in particular, her affair with the artist who belittled her by criticising her dress sense and making a cheap joke about her family's poverty. While taken singly, these incidents seem relatively unimportant, as a whole, they build up a picture of what has shaped Lucy and the things she most values.

Childhood memories are also evoked by her mother's visit and, although Lucy represses many of them, she reveals enough for the reader to comprehend the deprivation she suffered during her formative years. Frequently hungry and cold, Lucy lives in a garage until she is eleven years old and is deprived of anything which would teach her more about the outside world: books, TV and even the company of other children. Persecuted by classmates and teachers alike for being poor and dirty, she claims a single tree in a cornfield as her only friend. Loneliness becomes her default setting: an emotion that still sometimes overwhelms her as an adult, compelling her to strike up conversations with strangers. Lucy's narrative also touches, in the most veiled way, on the abuse she and her siblings suffer as children. While the moments she describes are of being locked in her father's truck for hours, her references to 'the Thing' hint at much more. Without providing the details, Lucy conveys how profoundly this abuse affected her when she confides that she often had the urge to run up to strangers in the street and beg them for protection.

Lucy's account also traces the effect the deprivation of her childhood had upon her sense of identity. Her tenuous sense of self as a child is highlighted by the fact that she doesn't even have a clear idea of what she looks like, as the only mirror in their home is hung so high she can barely see her reflection. As she grows older, her ambivalence about developing breasts becomes anxiety when her mother tells her she looks like the dairy cows in the neighbouring farm. Lucy manages to escape her narrow home life by earning a scholarship to college and then, later, moving to New York where she eventually achieves upper middle-class respectability. For many years, however, she feels a sense of inferiority and an unbridgeable chasm between her own experiences and those of the people she mixes with.

Lucy's sense of difference is a major factor in the breakdown of her first marriage. While William does his best to reassure her, Lucy finds it hard to believe that anyone can truly love her. She also becomes increasingly aware of the contrast between her own childhood and William's comfortable middle-class upbringing. The enormous gap between the two leads Lucy to believe that her husband can never truly understand who she is. As a result, she feels lonely in her marriage. While Lucy doesn't regret leaving William, the rift it causes with her daughters causes her a tremendous amount of pain. Significantly, when she remarries, it is to a man who has also suffered poverty and neglect as a child.

Closely connected to Lucy's search for identity is her dawning realisation that she is a writer. Lucy decides she wants to be a writer when she is a child after reading a book about a girl named Tilly who is "dirty and poor". Just as the book makes her feel less alone, Lucy hopes her own books will help others to feel less lonely. For Lucy, writing is also a therapeutic act of expression in a family where so many things cannot be spoken about.

Lucy's ambition to be a writer remains undimmed but she has difficulty admitting it to other people. Even when she has two stories published, she is dismissive of the achievement in front of others. While her friend, Jeremy, advises her that she must be 'ruthless' in the pursuit of her art, Lucy, at times, seems too uncertain of herself to follow this advice. Instrumental in Lucy's journey to truly believe that she is a writer is Sarah Payne. Sarah, a published novelist who comes from a similar background to Lucy, becomes a mentor, providing advice on writing and also epitomising what it is possible for Lucy to achieve. As Lucy gradually becomes more confident in her identity as a writer and achieves some success, she also becomes more confident as a woman, no longer feeling apologetic about her origins. This is nicely symbolised by her admission that she regularly shops at

Bloomingdale's and feels at home there.

Interestingly, as Lucy's sense of identity solidifies she realises that, while Sarah Payne initially inspired her, there are certain things about her old mentor that she does not want to emulate: namely her embarrassment when saying her own name and her tendency to hold something back in her fiction. When Lucy finally declares with authority, "This one is my story. This one. And my name is Lucy Barton", she shows that she has surpassed her mentor in her determination to express herself.

## **Lucy's Mother**

When Sarah Payne reads Lucy's account of her mother's hospital visit, she pronounces it to be a story about a mother's 'imperfect' love for her daughter. Sarah hits the nail on the head here, for at the heart of the character of Lucy's mother is a complex portrayal of maternal love which is felt but often withheld and never expressed.

Without ever explicitly blaming her, Lucy's account establishes many of her mother's failings as a parent. While failing to protect her children from their father's psychotic episodes and defending his behaviour, she also regularly lashed out at the children for no apparent reason. Offering no encouragement when Lucy goes to college, she seems to resent her daughter's new life and accomplishments, eventually causing Lucy to cease to visit her.

The appearance of Lucy's mother at the hospital in New York is extraordinary for two reasons: firstly, that she has braved her first flight to travel there, and secondly, that the gesture seems to demonstrate an intense love for her daughter that she has never previously revealed. Her devotion also seems to be confirmed by the fact that she never willingly leaves her daughter's side for five days and nights. While she never directly expresses her love and concern for her daughter, she demonstrates her feelings through telling gestures: the wiggle of a hand; the squeeze of a foot; the use of Lucy's pet name and, perhaps most poignantly, her willingness to wait for hours in a dark basement to be there when Lucy emerges from a CAT scan.

The love Lucy's mother feels for her daughter is also implicit in the stories she tells about the women of her hometown. While, on the surface, these stories are gossipy tales of others' misfortunes, they also serve a deeper purpose. Largely recounting the fates of women whose marriages have ended (through divorce or death), the stories seem to serve as both a warning and a preparation to her daughter who, Lucy's mother accurately predicts, will also have marital difficulties of her own. The desire to communicate something meaningful to her daughter is reflected not so much in what she says but in the uncharacteristically urgent way she says it, "as though a pressure of feeling and words and observations had been stuffed down inside her for years."

While it is clear that the intentions of Lucy's mother are good when she visits the hospital, the 'imperfect' nature of her love is also constantly evident. In a kind of coy courtship, she seems to seek greater intimacy with Lucy, only to retreat or withdraw altogether when she seems to have attained it. When Lucy asks her why she came to the hospital, she has the opportunity to express her love and concern, but instead simply replies that she came at the request of Lucy's husband. On another occasion, after building a rapport with her daughter as they discuss the women of Amgash, she abruptly falls silent and turns away when Lucy tries to tell her something about her own life. Similarly, after a breakthrough moment when she unexpectedly apologises to Lucy for failing to protect her from poverty and humiliation as a child, she again ruins the moment by claiming to have no memory of Lucy's long periods locked in her father's truck. Finally, and perhaps most inexplicably, after a devoted five-day vigil at her daughter's bedside, she abruptly announces that she is leaving just as Lucy is told she may require surgery. On each of these occasions we feel Lucy's hurt but also recognise how hard it is for her mother to break out of old behaviour patterns.

The imperfect nature of the love Lucy's mother feels for her daughter is most poignantly illustrated in her inability to verbalise it. One of the most moving moments in the novel is the scene in which Lucy closes her eyes and tries to coax her mother into admitting that she loves her. The emotion of this scene is later echoed when Lucy's mother responds to her daughter's letter (which tells her she loves her and will never forget her hospital visit) with a postcard of the Chrysler Building that reads, "I will never forget either." While Lucy is touched by the lengths her mother must have gone to in order to get hold of the postcard, she is also painfully aware of its omission. In both incidents Lucy's mother is given the perfect cue to tell her daughter that she loves her but cannot bring herself to do so.

While the narrative never offers a conclusive reason for the behaviour of Lucy's mother, there are a few clues to aspects of her life that may have shaped her character. Her claim that she never felt safe as a child and, therefore, learned to 'cat nap' suggests a history of abuse in her own childhood. Sarah Payne also suggests that an unhappy marriage may have been a factor, pointing out that her mother may have only stayed with her father, "because most wives did in that generation". When she is a child, Lucy notices that beatings from her mother usually only occur when her father is present. This suggests that her mother's outbursts of violence are part of a chain of abuse where wife-beating is the catalyst for child-beating.

A couple of anecdotes also provide a glimpse of the humiliation Lucy's mother has suffered due to poverty. The first is the story Lucy recounts about her mother losing her job at the local library. Lucy is surprised to learn that her mother once loved books (as there are none in the house) and finds out that her mother lost her job due to her lack of qualifications. In the second anecdote (told furiously by Lucy's mother) she sees a woman who resembles Marilyn Mathews from her hometown and tries to strike up a conversation but the woman snubs her. Significantly, both these stories take place in libraries and involve a humiliation which revolves around social status and class. Both experiences have the effect of making her feel inferior, and her knee-jerk reaction to the first incident is to stop reading and visiting libraries for many years. Through telling these two anecdotes, Strout provides a clue to why Lucy's mother refuses to acknowledge any details of her daughter's adult life. Through education, Lucy has gained access to a middle-class world she feels has always been denied to her. While many parents would be proud of this achievement, Lucy's mother clearly feels that, in doing so, her daughter has risen above her and placed a barrier between them. The fact that, as a writer, much of Lucy's world revolves around books, only serves to rub salt into the wound.

In addition to the factors of abuse and poverty, Strout also seems to suggest that the brusque manner adopted by Lucy's mother' is a form of self-protection from truths she cannot bear to face. While she refuses to talk about issues that cause her pain (her husband's psychotic episodes, her daughter's incomprehensible middle-class life), she also experiences apparent lapses in memory when it comes to recalling Lucy's childhood. This is particularly evident in the scene where Lucy uses a curse word and her mother comments that she has picked up bad language while living in New York. Lucy privately recalls that she regularly overheard much worse language when she was living with her parents, but her mother genuinely seems to have erased this from her mind. Similarly, when Lucy's mother claims that she cannot remember her daughter being locked in the truck as a child, her response appears to be truthful, although it is hard to believe. It isn't clear whether this erasure of uncomfortable memories is conscious on the part of Lucy's mother but it has clearly developed as a strategy to cope with the difficult facts of her life.

## **Lucy's Father**

A picture of Lucy's father emerges through Lucy's memories of childhood. As a girl, Lucy leaves in fear of 'the Thing': her father's episodes of erratic behaviour which range from aggression to extreme anxiety. As these episodes are never spoken about, Lucy doesn't realise until she becomes engaged to William that her father suffers from post-traumatic stress disorder, brought on by his experiences in World War II. This fact only comes to light when meeting William for the first time provokes an episode in her father and Lucy's mother finally explains that he had a "bad war". While the official story is that a German man almost killed her father, Lucy eventually learns that, in reality, her father shot two innocent German youths in the back and was haunted by the episode for the rest of his life.

Through Lucy's memories, Strout illustrates the way that her father responds to his trauma by traumatising his own family. While his inability to hold down a job contributes to their poverty, his unpredictable moods cause his children and wife to walk around on eggshells, in fear of his next episode. Two particular memories provide a glimpse of the kind of behaviour 'the Thing' entailed. The first is Lucy's recollection of being locked in her father's truck for hours and the second is the public humiliation of Lucy's brother, when he is forced to publicly parade in women's clothing as his father hurls insults at him. In addition to these memories the reader is also made aware that there are other incidents too painful for Lucy to share. Lucy provides a hint of what she may be omitting from her narrative when she describes her sense of recognition and shock when she hears the story of Janie Templeton, whose father suffered from PTSD and went around the house masturbating. The story evidently strikes a chord with Lucy as it comes very close to behaviour exhibited by her own father, raising the question of whether he sexually abused her.

While Strout makes the knock-on effects of his behaviour clear, her portrait of Lucy's father isn't entirely unsympathetic. This is most poignantly illustrated in the scene where, after publicly humiliating his son, Lucy later observes her father rocking him in his arms as they both cry. Here Lucy's father demonstrates shame for his behaviour and a sense of powerlessness. His evident love for his son suggests that his brutal behaviour was motivated less by homophobia than by a fear that a boy who displays feminine qualities will not survive in the world. This fear seems to be confirmed when Lucy later overhears her father telling her mother that he cannot allow their son to be sent to Vietnam. His conviction that the army will kill Lucy's brother demonstrates that he recognises the sensitivity in his son's nature, while his determination that he will not be drafted speaks of his fierce love.

Another incident that displays Lucy's father in a more favourable light is when he takes his daughter to the Black Hawk Festival. During the day Lucy is surprised to see her father watching the Indians dancing with obvious pleasure and is even more astonished when he agrees to buy her a candied apple. When Lucy finds the apple too hard to bite into, she is overcome with anxiety, fearing that her father will be provoked into an angry outburst. Instead, however, he eats the apple himself and Lucy loves him for not making her feel bad about it. Lucy remembers this incident as it is the only time she experiences a normal day out with her father. It provides a poignant glimpse of what their relationship might have been like without the existence of 'the Thing'.

When she is in hospital, Lucy still harbours "anger" and "disgust" towards her father and neither she nor her mother talk about him. When she finally meets him again, however, just before her mother dies, Lucy finds that her anger towards him has dissolved. Nevertheless, she is shocked at his insistence that there will be no funeral service for her mother. Shortly afterwards, Lucy's father also dies, making it clear that there should also be no service for him. This insistence upon a lack of fuss and public ceremony sadly underlines the belief of Lucy's father that he and his family are social outcasts who will not be mourned by the community.

## Lucy's Brother

Lucy's brother is never named. The first thing we learn about him is that, although he is in his mid-thirties, he is unemployed, still lives with his parents, reads children's books and chooses to sleep in a barn with pigs that are due to be slaughtered the next day. Given this information, readers might assume that he suffers from learning difficulties or mental health issues. As the novel progresses, however, we realise that his odd behaviour is a direct result of the poverty and abuse all the family's children suffered from in their childhood. While Lucy and Vicky go on to lead relatively normal lives (although suffering underneath it all), Lucy's brother is so badly damaged he is unable to function in the outside world. As his peculiarities are so obvious, his presence serves as a continual reminder of those things which the family do not talk about and try to forget.

Lucy remembers two incidents in particular which illustrate the sufferings of her brother as a child. The first was when she came across him, terrified and cowering, in the middle of a circle of boys who were beating him up. The second is the time when their father forces him to parade down the high street in women's clothing as a punishment for trying on his mother's clothes. The two incidents demonstrate the dual nature of the abuse he suffered: persecution by his peers and abuse from his father for being 'unmanly'.

The habits of Lucy's brother as a man poignantly illustrate his state of mind. In repeatedly reading 'The Little House on the Prairie' books, he tries to immerse himself in the fictional world of a happy, caring family. By sleeping with animals due to be slaughtered, he displays his empathy with creatures who are about to suffer.

Lucy keeps in touch with her brother after the death of their parents and, although he never moves from the family house, he takes a job working on farm machinery and proves to be a more dependable worker than their father ever was. This perhaps suggests that, once his parents are gone, he feels more able to take a small step into the outside world. Despite their frequent conversations, however, Lucy never learns anything more about his personal life.

## Vicky

Lucy's older sister, Vicky, goes on to live the kind of life that Lucy could have predictably fallen into without the benefits of education. When Lucy is in hospital, Vicky is thirty-four years old, has five children and lives only ten miles away from her childhood home. After their parents die, Lucy calls her sister regularly and listens to her rant about her lack of money and the fact that her husband never puts the toilet seat down. Vicky seems to feel both resentment that her younger sister has escaped a similar fate and a sense of entitlement to some of Lucy's good fortune. Lucy understands her sister's feelings and gives her money for the items she says needs for the children, even when the list includes yoga lessons.

The difficult relationship between Vicky and Lucy refutes the notion that sharing hardship brings siblings together. While Vicky and Lucy share similarly demeaning experiences at school because they are poor and dirty, the shared trauma divides them rather than bringing them closer. For both girls, witnessing the other sister's humiliation is an unwelcome reminder of their own situation.

## William

Lucy's first husband, William, at first appears to be a loving and considerate partner. Although he rarely visits his wife in hospital, his absences seem to be justified by the demands of work and his phobia of hospitals (as his father died in one when he was fourteen years old). He also goes to great expense to ensure that Lucy is comfortable, paying for a private room and for his mother-in-law's flight to New York. As the novel progresses, however, it becomes increasingly apparent that Lucy's marriage to William is disintegrating and that he has become romantically involved with the 'family friend' who helps with the children while Lucy is in hospital.

While William's infidelity is a factor in the break-up of the marriage, he is by no means entirely responsible. Through the glimpses Lucy provides of her marriage, William emerges as a sympathetic figure who genuinely cares for his wife. His tenderness towards Lucy is shown in small gestures (the way he calls her 'Button', his sadness in having to tell her that her mother hasn't passed on a message for her, etc.). While he recognises how badly his wife has been damaged by her upbringing, however, Lucy feels he is unable to fully understand her, as the chasm between their experiences is too great.

When they first meet, Lucy feels as if William's social background is not too far removed from her own, as his father came to the country as a German prisoner of war and, in her first marriage, his mother was a farmer's wife. When Lucy finally meets William's widowed mother, however, she is greeted by a graceful, middle-class woman who dresses well and is nothing like any farmer's wife she has ever met. For Lucy this evident disparity between their backgrounds comes as a shock. Conscious that William could have no concept of what her childhood was really like, Lucy feels unworthy of his love and William's protestations are unable to convince her otherwise. Eventually, it seems, he admits that his attempts to help Lucy are spurious: a decision reflected in his announcement that he no longer feels able to visit homeless shelters on Thanksgiving.

## **The Second Husband**

Although Lucy's second husband doesn't appear in the novel and is never named, Lucy reveals enough about him for the reader to understand why they are compatible. A professional cello player for the Philharmonic Orchestra, he shares Lucy's artistic streak and, even more significantly, grew up in great poverty with a 'crazy' mother who was incapable of showing her children love. Having realised that the gap between her own childhood experiences and that of her first husband was insurmountable, Lucy clearly chooses a second husband who will understand the physical and emotional deprivation she suffered as a child.

## Becka & Christina

Lucy is devoted to her two daughters and finds her separation from them while she is in hospital almost unbearable. Unlike her mother, she has no problem freely expressing her love for her children both verbally and through affectionate gestures. As a result, her relationship with them when they are small children is a good one. This bond with her daughters is, however, put under a great deal of strain when she leaves their father. Although, by this time, Becka and Christina are young adults, both are deeply affected by the separation and, for a while, refuse to see their mother. While the girls eventually soften towards their mother, it becomes clear that their relationship is never fully repaired when Lucy reveals that they have never stayed the night in her apartment, even though she has always kept a guest room specifically for this purpose.

The reaction of Becka and Christina to the divorce highlights one of the recurring themes in the novel. Although adults, they still retain childlike feelings about their parents. This is demonstrated when Christina reveals that, even though she has become fond of the new partners of both her parents, there is part of her that hopes that they die so that Lucy and William will get back together again. Lucy understands only too well how deeply her actions have hurt her daughters and suffers great guilt. As a result, the trauma she suffered as a child and the pain she has inflicted on her own daughters become inextricably linked. This is highlighted when Lucy cries out "Mommy" and doesn't know if she is calling for her own mother or echoing the cry of her own daughter when she saw the destruction of the World Trade Center.

## The 'family friend'

The 'family friend' first appears in the novel when she brings Lucy's children to the hospital to see her. While Lucy is grateful to see her daughters, she notices that the other woman hasn't washed the girls' faces or brushed their hair: an oversight Lucy puts down to the friend having no children of her own. Similarly, when she gets out of hospital, Lucy finds that the friend has made a terrible mess of Becka's hair by trying to cut gum out of it.

Lucy never reveals the name of the family friend and the title she gives her is shown to be ironic when she later reveals that

William's relationship with the woman is a contributing factor to her marriage break-up. William goes on to marry the family friend and Lucy finds it painful to hear her daughters refer to their 'stepmom': particularly as she remembers her apparent lack of mothering skills when she was looking after the girls.

Lucy's depiction of the 'family friend' is, of course, coloured by subjectivity. Whether she is really hopeless with children, or whether Lucy deliberately picks out details to suggest this is left for the reader to decide.

## **The Doctor**

While she is in hospital, Lucy forms a "deep attachment" to her "jowly-faced" Jewish doctor. Throughout her account, Lucy frequently mentions her love for the doctor which endures long after she has left hospital.

From the beginning, there is an unspoken rapport between Lucy and her doctor. Lucy feels that he wears "gentle sadness on his shoulders", possibly as a result of the deaths of his grandparents and aunts in German concentration camps. In return, the doctor seems to sense Lucy's sadness and takes a special interest in her recovery, visiting her at weekends and sending her for numerous tests, while only charging her for five hospital visits.

While it is possible for readers to come to the conclusion that they have romantic feelings for one another, this theory seems to be negated by the way they interact with each other. When the doctor kisses his fist towards Lucy, his parting gesture could be interpreted as impropriety. Taken in the context of all his other bedside mannerisms however (such as the way he places his hand on Lucy's brow to gauge her temperature), it is clearly an awkward gesture of paternal love. Meanwhile, when the doctor fails to visit her on Father's Day, Lucy envies not his wife, but his children.

For Lucy, the doctor offers the parental love and care she craved but never received as a child. She also realises that he is exactly the type of kindly stranger she hoped for when she imagined running up to someone in the street and begging them to rescue her from her home. Although the doctor never gets to the bottom of the reason for Lucy's illness, it becomes clear that his care contributes significantly to her process of psychological healing.

**Sarah Payne**

Lucy loves New York for its "gift of endless encounters". One of the most significant of these encounters is when she goes into an expensive clothes store and feels an immediate affinity with a 'ditzy'-looking older woman. On striking up a conversation with the woman, Lucy immediately likes her, feeling that her inner beauty is reflected in her face. Lucy asks the woman what she does for a living and she replies that she is "just a writer". When Lucy asks her name, she says with embarrassment and evident reluctance that it is Sarah Payne.

After her first encounter with Sarah, Lucy realises that she has read and enjoyed her novels. Motivated by her liking of the author and also her own desire to write, Lucy seeks her out, first going to a debate at New York Public Library where Sarah is speaking and later attending a writing workshop run by the author. Although Lucy only ever sees Sarah on a handful of occasions, her influence upon her as an inspirational mentor is extremely important. The more she gets to know Sarah, the more things she finds they have in common and there is a strong sense that both women recognise themselves in each other.

When Lucy observes Sarah's difficulty in saying her own name, she completely understands. Both women suffer from lack of self-esteem and have the tendency to belittle their creative talents in public. They also share an emotional sensitivity that makes it difficult for them to conceal their feelings (demonstrated in the exhaustion plainly reflected in Sarah's features during the writers' retreat). Most importantly of all, it becomes clear that they share similar backgrounds. Like Lucy, Sarah also grew up in a poor rural area. She also suffers from PTSD (illustrated by her extreme reaction when a cat jumps through the window), suggesting a shared history of childhood trauma or abuse. All these similarities help to strengthen Lucy's tentative belief that, like Sarah, she could also become a successful writer.

Sarah's praise of Lucy's work and writerly advice are also important factors in Lucy's development as a writer. Sarah assures Lucy that her work will be published and gives her writing class valuable advice about the importance of being unflinchingly truthful and holding nothing back in their fiction. She also tells them that, like all writers, they will each have only "one story" but will tell it over again in different ways. In these scenes, it seems likely that Sarah's wise advice reflects Strout's own opinion on the purpose of fiction, particularly her belief that the job of a fiction writer is, "to report on the human condition, to tell us who we are and what we think and what we do." In addition to her professional expertise, Sarah also offers Lucy something which is perhaps even more valuable. When she reads Lucy's accounts of her conversations with her mother, Sarah points out that, although the story combines "poverty and abuse", it is more importantly "about a mother who loves her daughter. Imperfectly." In making this point, Sarah helps Lucy to see past the hurtful behaviour of her mother to the love she undoubtedly felt for her.

It seems likely that Lucy's eventual success as a writer is the result of heeding Sarah's advice to hold nothing back in her work, as the many things she cannot say in her life are expressed in her writing. After the writers' workshop, Lucy never sees her again and Sarah doesn't write any more books. When she thinks about Sarah, Lucy reflects that she never discovered what Sarah's 'one story' was and, despite her advice to other writers, Lucy feels that she always withheld something from her work. While Sarah is a great inspiration, Lucy eventually moves beyond anything that her mentor achieves, both in her fiction, and in her eventual ability to claim her name and her story unapologetically.

## Jeremy

Jeremy is a sophisticated Frenchman who claims to be descended from French aristocracy and lives in the same apartment building as Lucy. He is also one of several people whom Lucy is "half in love" with. Significantly, he is the first person to see through Lucy's self-deprecating manner and identify her as an "artist". Perceiving the way that Lucy is divided between her domestic life and her creative life, he also advises her to be "ruthless".

Lucy feels that Jeremy understands her loneliness, prompting her to confess to him that she almost envies the ever-increasing number of young men with AIDS, as they at least have a sense of community. In an ironic twist, Lucy later discovers that Jeremy is a member of that fraternity himself. An intensely private person, he tells no one about his sexuality or his illness and Lucy only discovers the truth when she comes out of hospital and learns that he has died. The news of Jeremy's death leads Lucy to wonder whether the AIDS patient who stared at her intently in hospital could have been her friend. Although she knows that she could find out for sure, Lucy chooses not to, unable to bear the thought that she may have failed to recognise her friend at his loneliest moment.

## **Molla**

Other than Jeremy, Lucy's only other friend in the Village is Molla, a Swedish woman. Like Lucy, Molla felt neglected by her mother as a child and, when she had children of her own, found she was still suffering from unresolved emotions. Unlike Lucy, however, Molla finds it easy to talk about her experiences and emotions: a trait Lucy admires in her.

When Molla visits Lucy in hospital she talks about her usual subject (her hatred of her mother). This reminds Lucy of Sarah Payne's claim that we all have only 'one story'. Significantly, when Molla leaves she kisses Lucy on the head: a maternal gesture which Lucy's real mother noticeably neglected.

## **Mr Haley**

Lucy's sixth grade social studies teacher, Mr Haley, is one of several people Lucy always remembers for his kindness. He earns Lucy's eternal gratitude and love by lecturing the class on the evils of thinking that they are better than someone else when he spots one of Lucy's classmates making fun of her. He also demonstrates his dislike of persecution in any form when he teaches the class about the exploitation of American Indians by the first American settlers. At the end of that year, Mr Haley leaves the school and, in retrospect, Lucy realises that he was probably drafted to fight in Vietnam.

## **The Artist**

When she is in college, Lucy has a brief love affair with a professor who she refers to throughout the novel as 'the artist'. Although a minor character, the artist is a significant figure as he clearly reflects Lucy's self-esteem (or lack of it). As a student, Lucy's lack of confidence leads her to mistake the artist's arrogance for sophistication and brilliance. She is completely in awe of his "harshness" and intelligence and even admires his decision to forego having children in order to pursue his art.

From the reader's point-of-view, it is clear from early on that the artist is an unsympathetic character. It takes several significant incidents, however, for Lucy to come to the same conclusion. The first is a disparaging remark he makes about Lucy's clothes and the second is the time when he boasts that his shirt came from Bloomingdale's. Both these incidents set distant alarm bells ringing for Lucy, as she is surprised at the superficiality they seem to reveal. The final straw, however, is baked-bean-gate. After asking a string of intrusive questions about Lucy's poor upbringing, which are clearly driven by voyeuristic curiosity rather than empathy, the artist asks Lucy what her family usually ate. Too embarrassed to admit to molasses and bread, Lucy tells him they ate a lot of baked beans. It is the artist's response (an insensitive wisecrack about farting) which finally leads Lucy to the conclusion that their relationship has no future.

Years later, when her marriage is under strain, Lucy bumps into the artist at an art exhibition. From his gaze she realises that he is critically assessing the hastily chosen outfit she is wearing and is suddenly conscious of her lack of style. The incident shows that the artist still has the power to make Lucy feel inferior and causes her to reflect that the desire to feel superior to other people is one of the most unpleasant human qualities. Lucy's anger about this incident is demonstrated when, after becoming a published novelist, she receives a letter from the artist praising her work. Although she replies to every other letter that she receives from readers, she doesn't respond to his. Finally, however, after many years of frequenting Bloomingdale's herself, Lucy comes to think of the artist with fondness and wishes him well: a sign that her sense of self-worth is strong enough to brush off the feelings of inferiority he previously evoked.

### **Cookie, Toothache & Serious Child**

When Lucy's mother allocates each of the hospital nurses a nickname to describe their characteristics, it shows a surprising sense of humour on her part. Toothache, however, demonstrates that Lucy's mother has assessed her somewhat harshly when she notices that Lucy is sad and puts her arm around her: a gesture Lucy loves her for.

## Kathie Nicely

During her hospital visit Lucy's mother tells a number of stories about women from her hometown who experience marital problems. While she seems to introduce them naturally into conversation it becomes clear that, in telling these stories, Lucy's mother hopes to prepare her daughter for the problems in her own marriage.

One of the most memorable stories is that of Kathie Nicely: a mother-of-two with a wealthy husband who, according to Lucy's mother, "always wanted more". Kathie's comfortable life came to an end when she left her family for a man who promptly dumped her, claiming to be gay.

This story resonates particularly strongly with Lucy who becomes upset when she learns that Kathie's husband and daughters never forgave her. While Lucy cannot know, at this stage, that Kathie's story foreshadows the path her own life will take, her distress at Kathie's loneliness suggests that she may have an intuitive feeling about it. In later life, while Lucy seems to have finally rebuilt her relationship with her daughters after the divorce, she expresses deep sorrow that her daughters never stay over in her guest bedroom. While she doesn't blame her daughters for this decision, Lucy sees it as a sign that they haven't fully forgiven her for leaving their father and she wonders if Kathie Nicely's children feel the same.

## Mississippi Mary

When Lucy and her mother discuss Elvis Presley, the conversation prompts Lucy's mother to tell the cautionary tale of Mississippi Mary aka Mary Mumford. Like Elvis, Mary came from Tupelo and was raised in poverty. Her luck changed for the better, however, when she married 'the Mumford boy' who was not only the captain of the high school football team but also the son of wealthy parents. Mary raised five or six daughters and lived a charmed life until she discovered that her husband had been having an affair with his secretary for thirteen years. When she found out she had a heart attack. Lucy's mother points out that, although Elvis and Mary both went from being poor to being very wealthy, it didn't do either of them any good.

## Cousin Harriet

One of the many marital tales of woe told by Lucy's mother is that of Cousin Harriet. Already cursed with buck teeth and bad breath, Harriet experiences more bad luck when her husband drops dead. Left destitute, she struggles to feed and clothe her children and has to fight to stop them being taken into care.

In telling Harriet's story, Lucy's mother takes the opportunity to criticise her daughter. She describes Harriet's fearful nature as a child as "silly" and then adds that Lucy reminds her of Harriet in many ways, including that "silly fear" of hers and her tendency to "feel sorry for any Tom, Dick or Harry that came along." Here Lucy's mother shows the kind of brutal dismissal of sensitivity that Lucy evidently had to endure as a child.

## Abel Blaine

Although Lucy and her mother often have vastly differing opinions, they both agree that Harriet's son, Abel Blaine, is a wonderful person. Lucy remembers that, although other children used to make fun of his too-short trousers, Abel was always cheerful and radiated good-heartedness. He also taught Lucy the useful skill of hunting for food in the dumpster behind the cake shop.

Abel's story is one of the few with a happy ending, as Lucy's mother reveals that he went on to marry the daughter of his boss and now lives comfortably in Chicago. Lucy's mother compares Abel's triumph over adversity to a tree that springs up and flourishes in the middle of nowhere. This comparison echoes the single tree that Lucy is drawn to as a child, growing in the middle of a cornfield. Ironically, Lucy's mother doesn't seem to realise that the same could be said of her own daughter, who has also overcome adversity to lead a different kind of life.

## Dottie

Cousin Harriet's daughter, Dottie, also has bad luck with her marriage, as her husband runs off with someone he meets in hospital while having his gallbladder removed. Lucy's mother compares the situation to her daughter's and Lucy assumes that she is suggesting that she may run off with one of the hospital staff. In reality, of course, there are strong hints that it is Lucy's husband who is conducting an affair while his wife is in hospital. The ambiguity of the statement by Lucy's mother could suggest that she suspects William of infidelity.

Although Dottie's story seems to be one more example of a woman ruined by a bad marriage, it differs from the others in the final fate of its protagonist. Instead of being utterly defeated by her husband's betrayal, Dottie picks herself up and goes on to run a successful bed-and-breakfast business.

## Marilyn Mathews

When conversation with her mother turns to Marilyn Mathews, Lucy remembers that, although Marilyn always smiled kindly at her and never mentioned it when she saw Lucy and Abel rummaging through a dumpster. Marilyn, who also used to serve the family's free Thanksgiving meal at church, represents the kind of non-judgmental kindness that Strout celebrates in the novel. Her goodness goes unrewarded, however, as her childhood sweetheart returns from Vietnam with PTSD.

# DISCUSSION QUESTIONS

1/ How would you describe the tone of Lucy's narrative? How did it make you feel?

2/ The novel has a strongly autobiographical feel to it. How does Strout achieve this?

3/ Lucy's story is told in a non-chronological way to reflect her train of thought. Did you find this effective? What impact does this technique have on the reader?

4/ The plot of *Lucy Barton* can be summarised in a couple of sentences. With this in mind, what is it that drives the narrative forward? How important is plot to you when you are choosing a novel? Has reading this novel made you re-evaluate your ideas about the importance of plot?

5/ Discuss the dynamic between Lucy and her mother. Were there any moments between them that you found particularly moving or shocking?

6/ Lucy's mother tells her daughter a number of anecdotes about old friends and neighbours from their hometown. What purpose do these stories serve? Why is Lucy particularly affected by the story of Kathie Nicely?

7/ During the conversations between Lucy and her mother in the hospital, there are many omissions and deliberate silences. Discuss the subjects that the two women avoid talking about and their motivations for doing so.

8/ Lucy worries that her readers will not understand her mother's inability to say 'I love you' and insists that "It was all right." Is it really all right? Is love less valid if it is never verbally expressed? Did you feel any sympathy for Lucy's mother?

9/ Why is Lucy drawn to the statue of the starving man and his children in the Metropolitan Museum of Art?

10/ How would you describe the relationship between Lucy and her doctor? What does he represent to Lucy? How did you interpret the moment when he kisses his fist and holds it in the air before leaving Lucy's room?

11/ Lucy's doctor never gets to the bottom of what causes her illness following her operation. Do you think Lucy's illness may be psychosomatic? If so, what do you think has brought it on?

12/ Were you surprised to discover that Lucy's first marriage didn't work out? In hindsight, what clues does Strout include to indicate that all is not well between Lucy and William? Do you think it is entirely William's fault that their relationship fails?

13/ Why do you think Lucy doesn't tell the reader more about the breakdown of her first marriage and the circumstances of her second? Would you have liked more details?

14/ Discuss the way the author portrays loneliness in the novel. Is New York an antidote to Lucy's loneliness?

15/ When Lucy first sees Sarah Payne she feels drawn to her. Why do you think this is? What do the two women have in common?

16/ Sarah Payne believes that the job of a fiction writer is, "to report on the human condition, to tell us who we are and what we think and what we do." Do you agree that this should be the essential purpose of fiction? If so, does Strout achieve this aim in her novel?

17/ Other than Sarah, which characters does Lucy feel most at ease with? Do you think that most of us find it easier to connect with people who share similar life experiences to our own?

18/ Lucy describes a number of incidents in which she felt moved by the kindness of others. Discuss the characters who show Lucy kindness. Why do these seemingly small acts make such an impression upon Lucy?

19/ Lucy is interested in, "how we find ways to feel superior to another person, another group of people" and believes it to be, "the lowest part of who we are". What examples of this unpleasant human trait does she give in her narrative? Do you agree that it is a common human failing?

20/ How does the deprivation Lucy suffers as a child impact upon the adult she becomes? By the end of the novel does she make peace with her past?

21/ The traumas experienced by Lucy as a child are never described explicitly. Why do you think this is? What do you think happened to her?

22/ PTSD from his experience of World War II has a devastating effect upon Lucy's father and his family. How do these themes reverberate into Lucy's life as an adult?

23/ What is the role of Lucy's brother in the story? Why does he appear to be so much more damaged by his childhood than his sisters? How do the rest of the family feel about him?

24/ Discuss the relationship between Vicky and Lucy. Were you surprised that their shared experiences in childhood didn't make them closer? Why does Vicky seem so resentful of her sister? Why does Lucy feel that Vicky is entitled to all the money she sends her?

25/ Discuss the way Lucy's growing sense of herself as a writer mirrors her developing sense of herself as an individual. In what respect does Lucy exceed the achievements of her mentor, Sarah Payne?

26/ How does Strout demonstrate the unreliability of memory in the way Lucy tells her story? Are there any parts of Lucy's story that you suspect she misremembers?

27/ Sarah Payne says to the members of her writing class: "If there is a weakness in your story, address it head-on, take it in your teeth and address it, before the reader really knows." Are there any weaknesses in *My Name is Lucy Barton*?

28/ In a review of *Lucy Barton*, Laura Collins-Hughes praised the novel but criticised its title, suggesting that it sounded like "the recently discovered memoir of a steely Puritan whose 17th-century life makes an unfortunate slog of a read." Do you agree, or do you think the title does the novel justice?

29/ Would you describe *Lucy Barton* as 'women's fiction' or are its themes just as relevant to both sexes?

30/ Sarah Payne claims that all writers have only "one story". What does she mean by this and do you agree with her? If you were to write a novel, what would your 'one story' be?

# QUIZ QUESTIONS

1/ What routine operation does Lucy initially go into hospital for?

2/ What can Lucy see from the window of her hospital room?

3/ What is the name of the small rural town where Lucy grew up?

4/ What serves as Lucy's family home until she is eleven years old?

5/ Who or what does Lucy think of as her only friend when she is a child?

6/ For how long does Lucy's mother stay by her daughter's bedside?

7/ What is the name of the woman who, according to Lucy's mother, left her husband and children for a lover who turned out to be gay?

8/ Lucy's mother sometimes calls her daughter by a pet name. What is it?

9/ What nicknames does Lucy's mother give to the hospital nurses?

10/ In the hospital, what does Lucy do to try to coax her mother into admitting that she loves her?

11/ Which celebrity does Lucy's mother describe as "trash"?

12/ Where does Lucy first meet Sarah Payne?

13/ What does Jeremy say Lucy will have to be in order to be a successful writer?

14/ What phobia does Lucy suffer from and why?

15/ Why does Lucy's father take such a violent dislike to her first husband?

16/ What name does Lucy give to her father's psychotic episodes?

17/ When a cat jumps through the window at the writers' workshop, what question does one of the students ask Sarah Payne?

18/ What incident does Lucy believe marks the end of Becka's childhood?

## QUIZ ANSWERS

1/ An appendectomy

2/ The Chrysler Building

3/ Amgash

4/ Her great-uncle's garage

5/ The single tree that stands in the middle of a cornfield

6/ Five days

7/ Kathie Nicely

8/ Wizzle

9/ Cookie, Toothache and Serious Child

10/ Closes her eyes

11/ Elvis Presley

12/ In a New York clothing store

13/ Ruthless

14/ She is terrified of snakes after being locked in her father's truck with one when she was a child

15/ He reminds him of an innocent German youth he killed in

WWII

16/ The Thing

17/ The psychoanalyst asks her how long she has suffered from PTSD

18/ When they watch the destruction of the Twin Towers on TV

# FURTHER READING

### *Olive Kitteridge* by Elizabeth Strout

Strout's Pulitzer Prize-winning novel is really a collection of thirteen short stories, all set in the same New England town and all linked by the presence of the title character. In each story Strout recounts the hopes and thwarted desires of a different resident of the small fictional town of Crosby. Running through all these accounts (sometimes as a major character and sometimes only mentioned as an aside) is Olive Kitteridge, a formidable retired schoolteacher, notorious for her blunt and abrasive manner. On closer examination, however, Olive is not as monstrous as she first appears. Readers of *Lucy Barton* will see similarities between Olive and Lucy's mother as Strout peels away the layers of her protagonist's brusque exterior to reveal a woman who loves deeply but cannot express her emotions.

### *Left Neglected* by Lisa Genova

Sarah Nickerson is an American supermom who simultaneously manages a highflying career and three children like a military campaign. Her life changes irrevocably, however, when she is involved in a car accident and suffers a brain injury. Forced to hand over the reins of her highly efficient life to others, Sarah finds herself under the live-in care of the mother who neglected her as a child. Slowly, mother and daughter get to know each other and move towards some kind of reconciliation.

## *Dept. of Speculation* by Jenny Offill

This is a story of marriage, parenthood and female creativity told by an unnamed woman. Like *Lucy Barton* the novel is made up of fragmented domestic memories which, pulled together, provide a portrait of a life. There are also parallels to Strout's novel in the conflict the narrator experiences between being a mother and becoming a ruthless artist.

## *Mrs Dalloway* by Virginia Woolf

This novel recounts a day in the life of Clarissa Dalloway, an upper-class woman preparing for a high-society party in early twentieth century England. Written in a modernist stream-of-consciousness style, Woolf's classic is a more challenging read than *Lucy Barton*. The pattern of its language aims to exactly capture the scattered processes of human thought – and this can take some getting used to. Woolf's literary aims in this novel are very similar to Strout's, however, as both authors strive to capture the essence of what it is to be human by describing a series of mostly everyday incidents.

# BIBLIOGRAPHY

**Books**

Strout, Elizabeth. *My Name is Lucy Barton*, Random House, 2016

**Articles**

Hannah Beckerman. 'My Name is Lucy Barton by Elizabeth Strout review - powerful storytelling.' *The Guardian*, 2 February 2016

J.W. Bonner. 'Interview with Elizabeth Strout.' KIRKUS, 12 January 2016

Laura Collins-Hughes. 'My Name is Lucy Barton weaves a delicate balance.' 9 January 2016

Sarah Hampson. 'Review: Elizabeth Strout's *My Name is Lucy Barton* is an exploration of memory.' *The Globe and Mail*, 22 January 2016

Lily King. 'Elizabeth Strout's *My Name is Lucy Barton* review.' *The Washington Post*, 4 January 2016

Corrina Lothar. 'Book review: *My Name is Lucy Barton*.' *The Washington Times*, 11 February 2016

Claire Messud. 'Elizabeth Strout's *My Name is Lucy Barton*.' *The New York Times*, 4 January 2016

Connie Ogle. 'Review: *My Name is Lucy Barton* by Elizabeth Strout.' *Miami Herald*, 8 January 2016

**websites**

www.elizabethstrout.com

https://www.metmuseum.org/toah/works-of-art/67.250/

# ABOUT THE AUTHOR

Kathryn Cope graduated in English Literature from Manchester University and obtained her master's degree in contemporary fiction from the University of York. She is a reviewer and author of The Reading Room Book Group Guides. She lives in the Peak District with her husband and son.

www.amazon.com/author/kathryncope

Made in the USA
Middletown, DE
12 August 2018